Compliance Ma
Guidebook & Reference

By Lee Werrell
Chartered FCSI FISMM

Limit of Liability/Disclaimer of Warranty

While the author has used best efforts in preparing this report, they make no representation or warranties with respect to the accuracy or completeness of the contents and specifically disclaim any implied warranties. The advice and strategies contained herein may not be suitable for your situation. You should consult with a professional where appropriate. The author shall not be liable for any loss of profit or any other commercial damages, including but not limited to special, incidental, consequential or other damages.

© **Lee Werrell 2014** Property of the Publishers

All Rights Reserved. Contents and/or cover may not be reproduced or distributed in whole or in part in any form without the express written consent of the Publisher. Cover image courtesy of: www.freeimages.co.uk

Publishers: IYC Cubed Limited

Printed Edition 4: May 2014

Foreword: The Compliance Manager

The UK Compliance Manager is usually a unique position filled by individuals who sometimes divide their time between compliance as a CF10 or 11 (or both) and even sales as a CF30. Obviously larger organisations will have a designated compliance and possibly training and competence manager and this book is aimed to help all models. This book refers to the UK Financial Services Regime under the Financial Services and Markets Act 2000 and should not be interpreted for any other jurisdiction.

We will deal with a number of aspects of the role of the Compliance Manager concerning the regulator and the regulators current perspective and hotspots, Retail Distribution Review (RDR) changes and the introduction of the new regulators from 1 April 2013. Addressing the role of the compliance officer within the compliance function and identifying good and bad practice we will also lead onto discovering the impacts on compliance and identify certain areas that cause concern to most compliance professionals.

In the main I will try to keep the chapters short and packed with information, bullet points and ideas for you to use. If it applies to your business model, use it; if not, see if there is anything you can adapt to make your life a little easier and more structured. Otherwise, just accept that some frameworks will need different parts of the information, especially the larger they get.

Whilst this guide is designed to provide a medium level of information, it is not a newcomers "Compliance Manager's Guide". We have not, for example gone into the basics of financial promotions or suitability, completing fact finds or writing suitability reports as there is already help and guidance available at that level. It is assumed that you are already an established financial service professional and have been involved in compliance for at least two years. In that respect I do not dwell on the more routine aspects of the job, nor will I rely on anecdotal evidence of my own experiences, large or small, to labour any points.

Greater detail can be found in the Appendixes where you will find hyper-links covering Applicable AML regulations, The Bribery Act 2010 and Bibliographies for the main areas of the Compliance Manager's role.

Note: Compliance Consultants can often provide a better and more cost effective service than larger organisations as they have skilled staff to hand, have more experience per consultant and can assess processes and procedures, as well as governance and risk elements.

Remember: If you have any concerns regarding any compliance issues, please contact an independent consultant who is a member of the Association of Professional Compliance Consultants (APCC), recognised as a trade body by the FCA.

The Compliance Manager Guidebook
By *Lee Werrell* Chartered FCSI FISMM Cert PFS
Tel *0207 097 1434*
www.complianceconsultant.org

Contents

Contents 6

Chapter 1: The Regulatory Environment in the UK 9
    The UK Regulators 11
    A New Regulatory Dawn 12
        Consumer Credit Act Regulation 13
        Statutory Objectives 13
    Regulated Activities Order (RAO) 14

Chapter 2 The U.K.'s anti-money laundering regime 17
    Moving Forward With Money Laundering 20

Chapter 3: Authorisation and Other Regulations 21
        Principles 22

Chapter 4: The Function of Compliance 30
    So what is compliance? 30
    Who is responsible for compliance in your firm? 31
    The Compliance Manager 33
        Specific characteristics of a Compliance Manager 35

Chapter 5: Compliance benefits 38
    Client benefits 38
    Company benefits 38
    Costs of compliance 40
    So why do we do it? 41

Chapter 6: The Compliance Contract 43
    A Compliance Mission Statement 44
    The Compliance Charter 44

Chapter 7: Mapping Your Territory 47

Chapter 8: Rules Mapping 51

Chapter 9: Financial Products and Services 60
　Regulated activities 62
　Designated Investments 65
　Retail Investment Products (RIPs) 66
Chapter 10: Compliance in Support Functions 68
　Set Plan 69
　Ongoing Training 69
　Cause and Effect 69
Chapter 11: Regular Compliance Activities 72
　So what regular compliance activities do we need to consider? 73
　　Activity: Compliance culture and ethics 73
　　Activity: Compliance manual maintenance 75
　　Activity: Reviewing policies and procedures 77
　　Activity: Regulatory training 78
Chapter 12: Compliance Advisory Work..83
Chapter 13: Compliance with the FCA...92
　Conduct Risk 93
　The FCA's general enforcement powers..96
　Information, information, information..97
　So your name is in the frame...103
　So what Can They Do to You?..106
　The FCA and settlement 108
　Other Potential Outcomes...109
Chapter 14: Compliance Risk Assessment 111
Chapter 15: Regulatory Visit Preparation 121
　Early Planning for any assessment 125
　Preparing for the Review...130

Chapter 16: Compliance Activities 142
    Maintenance of your compliance manual 142
    Maintenance of compliance policies and procedures 144
    Annual compliance monitoring plan 145
    Risk management 146
    Compliance advisory log 146
    Regulatory contact log 147
    Complaint handling 147
    Training & Competency 148
    Approved Person Regime 148
    Management information 149
Chapter 17: AML activities 157
Chapter 18: Compliance with Senior Management 162
Appendix 1: Applicable AML Regulations 164
Appendix 2: Bribery Act 2010 188
Appendix 3: Bibliographies 193
    Compliance Oversight and the Compliance Function 194
    Conduct of Business and Client Assets 197
    Regulatory Approach to Risk Management 201
    Compliance and Ethics 204
    Anti-Money Laundering 208
    PRA Links 212

Chapter 1: The Regulatory Environment in the UK

Compliance cost has been an issue ever since the initial financial services act was implemented in 1988. And many financial institutions are still decrying the amount of involvement and resource the compliance department still entails. It is fair to say that there would be no compliance function compliance officers or what may seem to be a bottomless pit of costs had there been no regulatory system put in place and amended by various governments. As we all know the financial services community originally attempted self-regulation and whilst there were some successes in this area, predominantly within the city of London in the broking areas, financial advisers both tied and independent exploited the various loopholes incessantly. This excessive flouting of the self-regulatory guidelines led to customer detriment, confusion and mistrust of not only advisers but also the product suppliers that they represented.

Needless to say compliance was required under a robust, coherent and transparent framework to provide a consistency across the industry concerning the general public and their investments right through to corporate needs and indeed into the highflying investment bank world as well.

Whilst the various governments were keen to police the financial services world they were obviously insufficiently resourced to ensure a sufficient and adequate monitoring of all the business models, types and the multitude of variations therein; therefore the compliance department was born on a proportionate basis, funded and resourced internally according to the relevant size of institution it represented. This is not to say that the compliance function does not justify itself on its own terms but no business would ever have volunteered for such a wide ranging and seemingly powerful organisation to be involved with all the firm's processes and procedures. Therefore it could be argued successfully that the compliance department remains an agent of regulation and regulatory fashion and can only be successfully understood using the regulatory regime in the UK as our starting point.

The UK Regulators

Until recently, to the layperson it would appear that there was a single financial regulator known as the Financial Services Authority (FSA) and they operated from a single piece of regulatory legislation known as the Financial Services and Markets Act 2000 (FSMA). This is a simplistic belief that is as inaccurate as believing that the moon is made of cheese. In the UK there are numerous regulatory bodies including the FSA that cover financial services activities. The simplest ones to explain this diversity would perhaps be the Pensions Regulator and the Panel for Takeovers and Mergers (POTAM) as well as peripheral organisations such as the Office of Fair Trading (OFT), Information Commissioner (ICO) and other commissioners and related organisations with an interest into aspects of financial services. Although most regulated firms are based and work within the UK there are often regulatory developments, largely set by the European Union that will impact domestic legislation quite heavily over the next few years. Typical examples of these would be Basel III (interpreted in the UK parlance as Capital Requirements Directive IV or CRD IV) and the Markets in Financial Instruments Directive (MiFID) review known as MiFID II. US legislation can also affect US citizens living and working abroad as well as a potential impact on firms dealing with companies that may have international interests in countries under close scrutiny by the US authorities.

Global compliance regulation will not be covered in this book as it is a subject of its own and may only serve to confuse things.

The FSA certain statutory objectives imposed upon it under FSMA, but these have now ended as the FSA are no longer the regulatory body responsible for regulated financial firms in the UK.

A New Regulatory Dawn

On April 1st 2013 the FSA split into two regulatory bodies, the Prudential Regulatory Authority (PRA) and the Financial Conduct Authority (FCA) with a third body known as the Financial Policy Committee from the Bank Of England providing guidance in the matters of financial stability to both bodies.

The PRA is, in effect, a subsidiary of the Bank of England and responsible for promoting the stable and rational operation of the financial system through regulation of all insurers and investment banks.

Taking responsibility for regulation of conduct in retail is the FCA, which will look after retail and wholesale financial markets and the infrastructure supporting these markets. The FCA will also be responsible for the prudential regulation of companies that do not fall under the remit of the PRA.

The new system for regulating financial services in the UK, will involve a number of bodies, each with their own responsibilities and objectives:

- The FCA is responsible for ensuring that relevant markets function well, for the conduct supervision of financial services firms, as well as the prudential supervision of firms not supervised by the Prudential Regulation Authority (PRA).

- The PRA is responsible for promoting the safety and soundness of deposit-taking firms, insurers and systemically important investment firms.

- The Bank of England will be responsible for protecting and enhancing the UK's financial stability. It has primary operational responsibility for financial crisis management and is responsible for oversight of payment systems, settlement systems and clearing houses. It is also the UK's resolution authority

- The Financial Policy Committee (FPC), within the Bank of England, will be responsible for contributing to the Bank of England's objective of protecting and enhancing the stability of the UK financial system, and, subject to that, supporting the economic policies of the Government, including its objectives for growth and employment. It will focus on identifying, monitoring and managing risks to the system.
- Her Majesty's Treasury (the Treasury) has overall responsibility for the UK's financial system, the institutional structure of financial regulation, and the legislation that governs it, both domestic and international.

Consumer Credit Act Regulation

The FCA has transferred the responsibility for Consumer Credit regulation from the Office of Fair Trading to the FCA as from the 1st April 2014. This means that there will be increased requirements for firms as they make the transition to a more heavily regulated area. The new Handbook for Consumer Credit firms is "CONC" and links are provided in the Bibliography section.

As this progresses the FCA will work closely with consumers, the industry and Government to develop proposals for effective regulation that helps the market to work well and seeks to ensure the fair treatment of consumers.

Statutory Objectives

The legislation creating the FCA provides a step away from multiple statutory objectives to simply; "To ensure that the relevant markets function well". To support this, the FCA will have three *operational* objectives:

- To secure an appropriate degree of protection for consumers.

- To protect and enhance the integrity of the UK financial system.
- To promote effective competition in the interests of consumers.

The PRA's role as prudential regulator will be grounded in its two statutory objectives:

- To promote the safety and soundness of all the firms it regulates. This involves firms having resilience against failure and, in the event they do fail, or simply in the course of business, avoiding harm resulting from disruption to the continuity of provision of financial services. In promoting safety and soundness, the PRA will be required to focus primarily on the harm that firms can cause to the stability of the UK financial system.
- Specifically for insurers, to contribute to the securing of an appropriate degree of protection for those who are, or may become, policyholders.

Both of these objectives are underpinned by the principle that a stable financial system, which is resilient in providing the critical financial services the economy needs, is a necessary condition for a healthy and successful economy.

Regulated Activities Order (RAO)

The investment activities and products which the FCA are responsible for monitoring in sale and, in future, product development, are stipulated in the Regulated Activities Order 2001 (RAO) which can be found on the FCA website by inserting RAO into the search box. The activities that are currently regulated, defined in part to of the RAO comprise of;

- accepting deposits;
- issuing e-money;

- effecting or carrying out contracts of insurance as principal;
- dealing in investments (as principal or agent);
- arranging deals in investments;
- arranging home finance activities;
- operating a multilateral trading facility (MTF);
- managing investments;
- assisting in the administration and performance of a contract of insurance;
- safeguarding and administering investments;
- sending dematerialised instructions;
- establishing etc. collective investment schemes;
- establishing etc. stakeholder pension schemes;
- providing basic advice on stakeholder products;
- advising on investments;
- advising on home finance activities;
- entering into a home finance activity;
- administering a home finance activity;
- agreeing to do most of the above activities
- Specified investments are defined in part three of the RAO and comprise:
- deposits;
- electronic money;
- rights under a contract of insurance;
- shares etc.;

- instruments creating or acknowledging indebtedness;
- Suckuk (Sharia compliant debt instruments);
- government and public securities;
- instruments giving entitlement to investments;
- certificates representing certain securities;
- units in a collective investment schemes;
- rights under a stakeholder pension scheme;
- rights under personal pension scheme;
- options;
- futures;
- contracts for differences;
- Lloyd's syndicate capacity and syndicate membership;
- rights under funeral plan contract;
- rights under regulated mortgage contracts;
- rights under a home reversion plans;
- rights under a home purchase plan;

Rights to or interests in anything that is a specified investments listed, excluding "rights under regulated mortgage contracts", "rights under regulated home reversion plans" and "rights under regulated home purchase plans".

For full details of these specified investment types and activities please refer to Chapter 2 of the Perimeter Guidance Manual (PERG).

Inevitably all of the above activities will lend themselves to money changing hands or being exchanged for contracts, certificates or other membership evidence and that will ultimately lead to the risk of money laundering.

Chapter 2 The U.K.'s anti-money laundering regime

The process that criminals used to hide the illicit origins of their cash or other assets is known as money laundering. To effectively launder money the criminals have to place the criminally sourced monies or property into a large number of businesses or institutions that have a high turnover of the same asset. This means that companies using cash in large volumes such as taxis or minicabs, fairground or circus, and market traders would be typically targeted by criminals in an attempt to hide the source of the monies. Investment companies were always prime targets for depositing large amounts of cash or other securities in exchange for an investment plan that would be considered legal at face value. Early encashment of the plan, suffering large charges or fees, would be insufficient to deter criminals as a small return of clean money on their illicit gains is considered worthwhile. This process is called placement.

Once this process is started moving the deposited funds or investments through a number of complex transactions would then follow. The longer the trail the more likely the next institution will be to trust previous vetting. This process is long and arduous and can be extremely labour-intensive requiring any number of bribes and kickbacks to associates that facilitate this process means that even less pennies in the pound are eventually received by the criminal gang. For larger amounts and on an international basis criminals will undertake a series of international wire transfer is through jurisdictions with either a strong bank secrecy legislation or minimal anti money-laundering requirements to confuse anyone auditing the transactions. This process is called layering.

The final section required in the laundering process is after the complex layering stage has been completed and the origin of the funds has been extinguished. The proceeds can then be invested perfectly legitimately without fear of detection or the money may be used to set up further businesses to launder money in the future. This part of the process is called integration.

Organised criminals specialising devising even more imaginative intricate and lucrative ways to disguise their activities it is important that the vigilant compliance officer or adviser spots any errors, inconsistencies or anomalies and makes the appropriate report through their MLRO to the National Crime Agency (NCA) which superseded the Serious Organised Crime Agency (SOCA) in October 2013, and not attempt to track down the origins themselves. We will cover the problems of tipping off later in this book.

Some things to look out for may include;

- multiple third-party payments for which there is not a clear rationale;
- multiple transactions which do not appear to have any economic benefits;
- customers based in one country but using a bank from another with no apparent reason; and
- any difficulty in identifying the beneficial owners of an investment or deposit

A further area of money laundering has been extended to terrorist financing arrangements where terrorist organisations may;

- create, run or manage a legitimate business where the profits I used to promote terrorism;
- create and operate bogus charities often used to promote terrorist beliefs and causes;
- fund terrorist action or known terrorist activists;
- or simply to buy arms

The United Nations is behind a number of international conventions in the money-laundering and terrorist financing areas such as the 1988 Vienna Convention against drug trafficking and the UN Convention for the suppression of terrorist financing. The EU has also been an enthusiastic legislator against money-laundering with the third money laundering directive being the latest major initiative and including subsequent amendments. The UK has implemented its own AML and counter-terrorist financing legislation and has approached it on a guidance basis under the authority of the Joint Money Laundering Steering Group (JMLSG) guidance notes. This guidance provides a comprehensive level of help:

- Internal anti money-laundering infrastructure that firms should implement including staff training reporting suspicions etc.
- The actual requirement for Know Your Client (KYC) letting that firms should use in respect of customers and transactions.

The guidance elements of the JMLSG are comprehensive and would be ignored only by a full. The FCA has stated that it observes the JMLSG guidance notes as an indicator that a firm complies with the FCA's own anti-money laundering requirements. The AML requirements are applied broadly across many industries as well as under the FSMA regime and any firm should have a general awareness that is tested periodically for the benefit of Approved Persons as well as the firm concerned.

The legislation you need to be aware of are;

- The Anti-Terrorism, Crime and Security Act 2001
- The Money Laundering Regulations 2007
- The Proceeds of Crime Act 2002
- The Serious Organised Crime and Police Act 2005
- The Terrorism Act 2000 (as amended by the Anti-Terrorism, Crime and Security Act 2001).
- The Terrorism Act 2006

- The Terrorism (United Nations Measures) Order 2006
- Trade and Financial Sanctions Legislation

Moving Forward With Money Laundering

The FCA have stated that they will also devote more resources to ensuring the biggest retail and investment banks are complying with their legal and regulatory obligations through their Systematic Anti-money Laundering Programme, a cycle of in-depth reviews of anti-money laundering and sanctions systems and controls. They will make examples of firms who take unacceptable risks.

Chapter 3: Authorisation and Other Regulations

In order to conduct any regulated activity in the UK an individual or firm has to be authorised and submit an application for authorisation to the regulator. It is an offence to conduct a regulated activity in the UK unless you are an authorised person under reference only or exempt from its requirements. This is known as the general prohibition.

The various ways of gaining authorisation are;

- obtaining permission to carry out regulated activities under part 1V of FSMA;
- exercising passporting rights under a relevant EU directive (EEA passport rights); or
- exercising the rights under the Treaty of Rome (treaty rights)
- There are also various categories of person subject to the regulations:
- individuals working for regulated firms;
- individuals working for themselves (one-man bands);
- regulated firms themselves;
- Recognised professional bodies (accountants, solicitors etc.);
- Collective investment schemes; and
- Clearing-houses or exchanges

If you are regulated by the FCA and PRA, or are applying for authorisation as a dual-regulated firm, you will not have to make duplicate applications to both regulators. You will get a single decision from either the FCA or PRA that reflects the decision of one or both regulators as appropriate.

• All paper applications for dual-regulated firms should be made to the PRA.

• All paper applications for FCA-only regulated firms should be made to the FCA.

• The regulator's Online Notifications and Applications (ONA) submissions will be automatically routed to either the FCA or both the FCA and PRA.

Principles

As we are all aware the FSMA requirements have been translated into the FCA's Handbook of rules and guidance. In recent years the FSA had moved towards more principle based approaches to regulation which has been the content of debate for a number of years. In the UK we have been used to working with a rules-based supervisory regime since 1988 however times are now changing and firms are encouraged to ensure their business is conducted appropriately with the relevant management information showing the business principles a complete picture of measured activity. Due to the recent 2008 global banking debacle the movement towards MPBR has slowed but nobody knows how the future will pan out and after the new regime of the FCA/PRA has been fully implemented and firms start to operate their businesses as businesses, the relaxation of various sections of the rulebooks is potentially likely to occur.

Having high-level principles a role to play in regulation is not new to the UK. The Securities and Investment Board (SIB) introduced 10 high-level statements of principle in 1990 and these were often cited in disciplinary actions. The FSMA saw the introduction of statutory objectives mentioned above, which serve as the FCA's guiding principles in terms of framework and definition. The FSMA also saw the introduction of the seven principles of good regulation that the FCA must comply with and the regulated firm's 11 FCA principles for business and the parallel implementation of the seven statements of principle for approved persons.

To remind you of the 11 principles for business they are as follows;

1. Integrity

A firm must conduct its business with integrity.

2. Skill, care and diligence

A firm must conduct its business with due skill, care and diligence.

3. Management and control

A firm must take reasonable care to organise and control its affairs responsibly and effectively, with adequate risk management systems.

4. Financial prudence

A firm must maintain adequate financial resources.

5. Market conduct

A firm must observe proper standards of market conduct.

6. Customers' interests

A firm must pay due regard to the interests of its customers and treat them fairly.

7. Communications

A firm must pay due regard to the information needs of its clients, and communicate information to them in a way which is clear, fair and not misleading.

8. Conflicts of interest

A firm must manage conflicts of interest fairly, both between itself and its customers and between a customer and another client.

9. Customers: relationships

A firm must take reasonable care to ensure the suitability of its advice and discretionary decisions for any customer who is entitled to rely upon its judgment.

10. Client's assets

A firm must arrange adequate protection for client's assets when it is responsible for them.

11. Relations with regulators

A firm must deal with its regulators in an open and cooperative way, and must disclose to the FCA appropriately anything relating to the firm of which the FCA would reasonably expect notice.

Seven Statements of Principle for Approved Persons

The seven statements of principles for approved persons have a dual function insomuch as the first four apply to all approved persons, and the last three apply to those who have a significant influence over the business.

Statement of Principle 1

An approved person must act with integrity in carrying out his controlled function.

Statement of Principle 2

An approved person must act with due skill, care and diligence in carrying out his controlled function.

Statement of Principle 3

An approved person must observe proper standards of market conduct in carrying out his controlled function.

Statement of Principle 4

An approved person must deal with the FCA and with other regulators in an open and cooperative way and must disclose appropriately any information of which the FCA would reasonably expect notice.

Statement of Principle 5

An approved person performing a significant influence function must take reasonable steps to ensure that the business of the firm for which he is responsible in his controlled function is organised so that it can be controlled effectively.

Statement of Principle 6

An approved person performing a significant influence function must exercise due skill, care and diligence in managing the business of the firm for which he is responsible in his controlled function.

Statement of Principle 7

An approved person performing a significant influence function must take reasonable steps to ensure that the business of the firm for which he is responsible in his controlled function complies with the relevant requirements and standards of the regulatory system.

Bearing in mind that the reader of this book is likely to be an experienced person within a firm we will not spell out the structure of the FCA Handbook, will not describe the money advice service run by the FCA nor will we delve into specific roles for regulated professional bodies.

A bibliography of links pertaining to various elements of the FCA Handbook's can be found in Appendix 3.

PRA Approved Persons Changes

On taking over their role, the PRA have announced that they will be making key changes to the Handbook for PRA Approved Persons which means that:

Statements of Principle issued by the PRA will apply to:

(i) PRA approved persons and persons approved by the FCA to perform a significant-influence function at a dual-regulated firm; and

(ii) the performance by such persons of any activity which could be a significant-influence function, insofar as it relates to the carrying on of a regulated activity by the firm which originally sought the approval;

The PRA's APER **will not** include **Statement of Principle 3**, which covers market conduct; and **Statement of Principle 4 is amended** to make clear that the PRA could take action against a person for failing to disclose to the FCA something that the FCA could reasonably have expected notice of.

The current Statement of Principle 4 states "*An approved person must deal with the FCA and with other regulators in an open and cooperative way and must disclose appropriately any information of which the FCA would reasonably expect notice.*"

Full details can be found at
http://fshandbook.info/FS/html/PRA/APER

Transitional arrangements for approved persons (SUP TP)

As set out above, the PRA will now approve applications for a larger number of controlled functions. This affects the detail of the transitional arrangements, but these will still follow the key principles set out in Chapter 3 of PS 15/5 "*Feedback on Regulatory Reform proposals relating to the FCA Handbook* ". All existing approvals will be 'grandfathered' to whichever of the PRA or FCA will specify that controlled function in its rules after legal cutover, without the need for any action by firms or their approved persons.

Where there are changes between the old FSA framework of functions and the new PRA and FCA framework firms will not be required to take action to switch existing people to the new framework of functions while they remain in their current role.

The role of approved persons and those who may be accountable within firms is under constant scrutiny and the regulators are considering wide-reaching changes in the near future.

FSA controlled function	FCA controlled function into which approved person transitioned	Firms to which transitional relates
Director function (CF1)	Director function (CF1)	All firms
Non-executive director function (CF2)	Non-executive director function (CF2)	All firms
Chief executive function (CF3)	Chief executive function (CF3)	FCA-authorised persons only
Partner function (CF4)	Partner function (CF4)	All firms
Director of unincorporated association function (CF5)	Director of unincorporated association function (CF5)	All firms
Small friendly society function (CF6)	Small friendly society function (CF6)	All firms

Table 1: FSA controlled functions transitioned to the FCA

Apportionment and oversight function (CF8)	Apportionment and oversight function (CF8)	All firms
Compliance oversight function (CF10)	Compliance oversight function (CF10)	All firms
CASS operational oversight function (CF10A)	CASS operational oversight function (CF10A)	All firms
Money laundering reporting function (CF11)	Money laundering reporting function (CF11)	All firms
Systems and controls function (CF28)	Systems and controls function (CF28)	FCA-authorised persons only
Significant management function (CF29)	Significant management function (CF29)	All firms

Customer function (CF30)	Customer function (CF30)	All firms
Benchmark Submission Function (CF40)	Benchmark Submission Function (CF40)	All firms
Benchmark Administration Function (CF50)	Benchmark Administration Function (CF50)	All firms

Chapter 4: The Function of Compliance

Compliance is effectively still a new and young profession and sometimes takes explaining to members of the general public who politely ask "what do you do?" Many people working within a compliance department of larger firms may feel they know all there is to know about compliance within their particular remit, however for the effective Compliance professional to stand out from the rest; they have to know a lot of things about a lot of areas.

There are various buzzwords surrounding compliance which inevitably confuse people both within the support functions and in the front, middle or back office such as compliance function, compliance department, a culture of compliance, compliance manager, and compliance officer. These words mean different things to different organisations and it is usually a generalised or woolly definition that will accompany the role as in most firms there is no definitive list of what a compliance manager or officer has to do, needs to do or should be seen doing.

So what is compliance?

To understand the world of compliance we have to start with a clear vision of what compliance is and the part it plays within the firm. To obtain a robust and sensible definition we have to distil the terms used in the various legislation and guidance to define our own concept. Add to the mix the need to explore the elements within compliance and it soon becomes apparent that the compliance manager is all things to all people.

The definition within any standard dictionary will provide a very broad definition regarding adherence to rules or the suchlike. We understand other industries where safety is considered then compliance means in-house policies conforming to a structure or a standard of operation to eliminate potential hazards.

The definition from the Basel committee on banking supervision in 2005 described compliance risk as;

"the risk of legal or regulatory sanctions, material financial loss, or lost your reputation a bank may suffer as a result of its failure comply with laws, regulations, rules, related self-regulatory organisation standards, and codes of conduct applicable to its banking activities (together, compliance laws, rules and standards)"

This definition is obviously high level and specific to the banking fraternity. But we could translate in refining the description to something more usable in everyday life such as;

"We define compliance within our firm as the function of identifying relevant legislative, regulatory and best practice requirements and then implementing the required changes to our systems and controls to facilitate adherence to these obligations on an ongoing basis."

Having defined your own interpretation of the definition of compliance brings us to the next question and the final part of understanding compliance within a financial services firm.

Who is responsible for compliance in your firm?

Unlike IT, finance or administration the question of who is responsible for compliance in your firm has many answers. It is not simply a case of the compliance officer being responsible for compliance within the firm as compliance is a far reaching discipline and like risk, the responsibility for the attainment of compliance rests with the entire staff.

It could be argued that the compliance department should not exist in any firm, as compliance being the responsibility of the entire staff would relegate the monitoring of compliance to internal audit, in larger firms, or the executive function in smaller firms.

The regulators principles of good regulation state "a firm's senior management is responsible for ensuring that it's business complies with regulatory requirements" and the FCA's Enforcement Guide (EG - found at http://media.fshandbook.info/Handbook/EG_FCA_20130401.pdf 2.31): Senior Management Responsibility states "The FCA is committed to ensuring that senior managers of firms fulfil their responsibilities. The FCA expects senior management to take responsibility for ensuring firms identify risks, develop appropriate systems and controls to manage those risks, and ensure that the systems and controls are effective in practice."

In fact if you scoured the FCA Handbook's you would find that it does not state in any handbook that the compliance officer or the compliance department are "responsible" for compliance. You'd be hard-pressed to find any official regulatory references to anyone called the compliance officer. This demonstrates that only in the financial services world could we have such an ill-defined role giving rise to a massively resourced profession within financial institutions across the country that we all know as the compliance industry.

To argue the semantics of this point may very well provide many hours of discussion over coffee, or a beer after work within the larger financial institutions and their compliance staff, but for the majority the compliance officer is usually a member of the senior management, directors or owners and therefore partly ultimately responsible to his peers and the regulators accordingly.

Running a compliance department can in some cases be likened to dancing amongst moving blades whereby you need to provide advice and guidance to senior management as well as ensure that your firm is run efficiently and smoothly and ensuring that they are not tempted to bypass you and make ill-informed regulatory decisions in your absence. It is a good idea at an early stage to ensure that everybody within the firm understands even though you may be accountable as the compliance manager or officer, and you may or may not consult other members of staff regarding the effective implementation of rules and regulations, that ultimately everybody is responsible for compliance within the firm.

In some firms, the relationship with the regulator is jointly handled with the firm's general counsel or legal representative. However, in most firms, not only is the Compliance Manager busy with the day-to-day compliance activities, owning the relationship with regulators, developing the compliance and regulatory framework within the firm and providing regulatory guidance and advice to the members of the firm, as a member of senior management they are also responsible for ensuring the compliance culture is embedded throughout the firm's infrastructure and are assessing and monitoring the activities of the compliance department for adequacy and appropriateness.

The Compliance Manager

Acting as the Compliance Manager or officer carries with it the heavy burden of responsibility including;

- developing a thorough understanding of the firm they work for and the entirety of regulatory impact upon the firm

- determining the best practice standards from across the industry and marrying them up with adequate regulatory and legislative requirements to provide a working, compliant sales model

- identifying how best they can apply requirements and practice standards that do not restrict growth or innovation would operate within the regulatory framework

- clearly documenting both the ways they intend the firm to maintain compliance and the methods of monitoring, assessing and appreciating measures which may involve in drafting manuals, policies, procedures, work plans, scripts, newsletters, bulletins, Internet attachments etc.

- Effective delivery of training and awareness activities to ensure that all staff are aware they need to do in order to comply with the regulations and to prove that they are up to date with the latest developments
- keep appraised of regulatory developments and changes that not only currently impact their firm will also future impacts on the radar screen and the necessary changes to their framework
- implementation of remedial action where instances of non-compliance or other problems that are identified require satisfaction
- conducting file reviews, training and competence assessments and monitoring sales activity to ensure a consistent, compliant and fair approach
- engaging in regulatory reporting to meet specific requirements such as RMAR or changes through the ONA system for personnel authorisations
- measuring, assessing and identifying compliance risks in order to be able to assess the impact and likelihood of particular risks materialising including understanding the risks, consequences, adequate controls and mitigation plans
- providing adequate, robust and coherent management information to all the senior management so that they can execute their management responsibilities compliantly and correctly
- and finally, become a confidante, friend, adviser, agony aunt and consultant on all things regulatory

We will cover these particular activities in further detail throughout the text of this book.

Specific characteristics of a Compliance Manager

As a compliance manager you will undoubtedly have firm ideas of how compliance should be run within your specific firm. It is also vital that you're aware of your own strengths and weaknesses and ultimately your own personal development with regard to people skills so that you can easily deal with all levels of individual within your organisation.

So what is a good compliance manager look like? What does a compliance manager need to aspire to? Does having a mug with "best compliance manager ever" stenciled on it count for anything?

The attributes of an award-winning Compliance Manager must surely for the list that would make any dating agency proud. I will not attempt to list these in their entirety however certain elements need to be present for the reasons that follow.

Confident: as compliance manager we should not be intimidated by anybody who has a loutish approach or try to intimidate anyone who will not bend the rules to suit them. Additionally you must also be confident enough to challenge the status quo and make waves at the highest levels of the firm if it is not clear or apparent that compliance has been adhered to.

Training delivery: being able to put across the compliance message in the firm, clear and positive way, explaining the rationale and necessity for everyone as a whole plays a major part in the Compliance Manager's make up.

Communication: to be able to communicate with people of all levels within the firm or organisation is of critical importance as anybody who seemed aloof or inappropriately insincere will not engender the respect needed.

Regulatory universe: understanding the entire impact of the various regulators that affect our firm does not only give you a sound grounding but should also provide you with a clear understanding of where the rules originate and why they have been brought about.

Attention to detail: this is particularly important for interpreting new rules monitoring analyses and investigations and also involves your inventiveness and creativity so that you do not end up with a "no", but can provide alternative solutions to any situation.

Gravitas: you must be credible when you say yes or no. Dithering or prevaricating will not get you the respect you need to control a compliance department or framework within the firm, but whatever your answer, people will know you have the background experience and common sense approach that they can rely on and more importantly a consistent format of explanation.

IT and report writing skills: being able to use IT systems competently and efficiently pays dividends in not only report writing but in analyses of data and preparation of management information for the senior management as well as the regulatory reporting requirements of tomorrow that will become more web-based.

Decision making: a knack to learning and understanding new situations so that you can make quick decisions or, with confidence, not to make quick decisions will stand you in good stead.

Diplomacy: a key element to people skills is the art of negotiating and persuading. A compliance manager uses threats intimidation and bullying tactics is not usually a compliance manager for very long.

Patience: is not only a virtue but a keen attribute to develop.

Enthusiasm: without this, working as a compliance manager becomes a chore, and you soon tire of all the grief, gripes, moans and groans associated with people.

Working as a compliance manager, officer or consultant has its own rewards much like those who follow a vocation in teaching or nursing. Whilst compliance in itself is not rocket science, bad sales practices over the years from shaky and sensationalist leaders in supposed sales psychology, have created a raft of issues in their delivery that alone may not amount to a great deal of harm. The problem is when treating customer's fairly, these "techniques" and "sales management methods" collectively can mislead or detract a potential client who may then be confused about the message delivered and ultimately act in a way contrary to their best interests.

Chapter 5: Compliance benefits

Client benefits

Fundamentally the detailed regulatory compliance rules are aimed at ensuring that customers get a fair deal and are fully aware of all risks, benefits and challenges involved in the execution of their order or investment planning. Basic business sense would dictate that if we serve our customers well, they are likely to remain happy and less likely to complain or sue us for compensation.

Improve systems including the customer focused rules of reporting, customer agreements, notifications etc. mean that the service you provide is more transparent to the onlooker and therefore more credible and dependable.

By maintaining a firm's integrity and fairness to its clients not only increases loyalty will also lead to referrals of other quality clients and for a long term view provide a sustainable competitive advantage.

Ultimately the fair treatment of customers, transparent procedures and processes as well as full disclosure and explanation will need to increase profit and maintain the firm as a supplier of the financial services long into the future.

Company benefits

Not all regulatory requirements are directly concerned with improving the customer buying experience; many are aimed at enhancing the firm's internal systems and controls to improve the efficiency of the firm.

It has been long understood that a well-run, well-managed and a robust firm with effective and proportionate governance systems in place helps identify accountability at all levels and ensure correct apportionment and oversight of the controls in place. This then leads to a wealth of management information (should the correct key performance indicators be identified) to facilitate a successful risk and compliance model feedback loop.

Compliance and efficient internal arrangements means that you are less likely to have to pay out money in fines or to find additional resource to administer your procedures and processes. This also is likely to mean less litigation and the general efficiencies will obviously lead to lower costs. The stronger and more robust systems and controls in place more often allow for greater leniency under the regulatory capital regimes as long as these can be proven. As with the unsung heroes of compliance saving companies from disaster there is never usually any method that you can clearly say directly saves the company money like a solid, well invested risk framework.

Reputation is becoming increasingly important in the financial services world and the FCA have stated they will be looking at ways that can best measure a firm's reputation and mitigate any negative press it may receive. Compliance involvement in the systems and controls for both business continuity planning as well as crisis management planning can ensure minimal negative and maximum positive emphasis on any reputational impact.

With the increased use of social media and the Internet generally, a red flag is waved toward the regulators every time your company is mentioned in a bad light. If you can show that your systems and controls are effective whenever these instances occur it is more likely that you will have a light touch approach from the regulators if they were to make enquiries.

The main benefits to your firm can and often will be hidden amongst the commercial crises that form the peaks of the waves of normal operation within any firm. This is why it is vital to keep a log of all advice, questions, queries, recommendations and other responses that you may come across on a day-to-day basis. An additional benefit of keeping this log is that it provides an audit trail as well as justification for the effectiveness of the department and shows the involvement within the culture of the company. Nobody cares how many regulatory consultation papers you may have read in the previous 12 months, but publishing highlights and extracts from them with an easy to follow narrative, summary of impact and general circulation amongst the firm will not only increase people's knowledge of the regulated activity but also provide you as the compliance manager, an avenue of communication with your colleagues.

Your knowledge of rules and the rulebooks combined with knowing the regulatory hotspot and the industry friction areas gives us the information to guide our firm through the annual business plan in a compliant way with little expectation of regulatory scrutiny, poor reputation or other such associated compliance horrors. Operating a clear, straightforward and effective complaints department helps protect our firm from vindictive and irresponsible clients who sometimes enjoy malicious acts that will waste management time and cause unrest among staff. This also provides another area for the Compliance Manager to justify the work that is conducted by providing good management information on financial promotions and complaints, elements which are often taken for granted or overlooked by the rest of the staff unless they are directly involved.

Costs of compliance

Let's not kid ourselves, about the benefits of regulation and compliance, as we all know that the adaption and implementation of these elements undoubtedly has significant cost and where these factors are being applied to no obvious benefit will attract serious criticism. It's often best to have some form of response whenever anybody throws a curveball at you regarding the cost of compliance.

There are obviously going to be staff costs, i.e. salary, bonus, pensions or other benefits, office space, desk and computer equipment, fax machines, printers, cabinets, IT programs, designated folders or hard drives, training budget and attendance of regulators training days as well as all the indirect costs.

Indirect costs can be attributed from training where your advisers are not doing their job, i.e. making sales or building relationships, performing remedial work on cases you've rejected on compliance grounds, additional compliance administration and anti-money-laundering requirements, T & C assessments as well as any other remedial exercises if you have uncovered a regulatory problem where cooperation and assistance from the operational staff will be required.

So why do we do it?

Everything mentioned to this point should have made perfect sense on a variety of levels, so why do Compliance Managers have such a hard time or bad press? Why are some Compliance Managers so unpopular? What are these chips that people have on their shoulders about compliance?

Obviously perception plays a big part in the image of the firm's compliance department. People do not generally like to be told what do and all too often Compliance Managers are seen to be saying "don't do this, don't do that", and are likened to fishwives of the industry. A healthy compliance culture and a well-run department will head off most of this criticism and sniping as we've already seen in the good compliance areas described.

There cannot be any criticism on a Compliance Manager's pay as this hardly compares to those that he shepherds. Whilst not excessive, a Compliance Manager's pay should reflect the additional responsibilities as if they make a wrong call the weight of regulatory compliance, regulators and the law will descend in short order on their shoulders. And any Compliance Manager should be able to take solace in the fact that some regulators have it worse, and the odd few even lose their life after making unpopular speeches in public.

So why do we do it? Because we feel we can make a difference. Working in compliance makes you understand the industry working that much better. A good compliance manager understands the entire process within the firm they operate, from cradle to grave. It is a very people centred role that enhances your public relations skills as well as give you the opportunity to forge relationships with all levels of people covering all manner of issues, across the firm. There is the opportunity to specialise such as financial crime, financial reporting and controls, monitoring, training and competence, training, KYC, computer-based systems, surveillance and forensic investigation but for most firms we tend to do a bit of "all of the above".

There are those of course who consider the ethical challenge to be more interesting, and indeed there are more who involve themselves in strategy and business planning for new products and service offerings. There is generally a move between the marriage of Governance, Risk and Compliance (GRC) and many pundits to more than match those who follow this path.

For those of you who want to develop your project management or problem-solving skills, compliance can be very fulfilling and enables you to be more creative when considering regulatory dictates.

All in all the Compliance Manager does their best in all cases of identifying regulatory change and requirements and implementing them to the best of their efforts to work within the firm, to enable their colleagues to grow the business and provide future security for all those within the firm.

Chapter 6: The Compliance Contract

In the next five chapters we will cover guidance on the key elements within your world and the fundamentals of identifying the areas of concern as well as a framework to identify emerging issues. Once you have a handle on all of the compliance requirements within your firm it will be time for you to explain it to everyone else. The more positive ways and number of things that you can say are working within the compliance arena the more likely you will get support and buy in from the rest of the firm.

If you are starting from new you have to make sure that the board and senior management buy in to the extent of your responsibilities and the nature of your activities. Quite often the actual job description for anyone in your position is quite vague and subjective. It is therefore up to you to define not only your role and responsibilities, but also to mark the boundaries. Typically this may mean compiling or amending the compliance mission statement and when it is complete it should be promulgated at every opportunity. Reference to this document should be made in opportune moments to draw people's attention to the fact that it exists and is a credo for the department. To provide additional comfort to the rest of the firm as well as provide a service level agreement for the department to provide services to the firm, you should consider preparing an official compliance charter. Lastly we should consider conducting training so that staff are aware of what the compliance department does and the ways in which you can help them. You should prepare a schedule of compliance e-mail bulletins as mentioned earlier regarding regulatory developments or even to highlight compliance issues such as the top three challenges with examples, top five common mistakes with financial promotions submissions or even common complaints. Obviously this list can go on and on but for most Compliance Managers this should cover the majority of what they need to do.

A Compliance Mission Statement

The compliance mission statement should provide a succinct definition of the fundamental aims of the department and can in fact be split into two for any internal and external audits. Internally this will describe to any team member what priority tasks and focus methodology is to be used. Externally a more positive expression briefly covering how you propose to support the rest of the business without compromising yourself, the department or the level of trust the rest of the staff may have in you. The key here is to make the least possible subjective statements as with all of these, they are open to interpretation and could well come back to haunt you.

The Compliance Charter

The compliance charter expands the concepts within the mission statement and can be used to serve both as a promotional piece and a high level contract for services between the compliance department and the rest of the firm. Senior management should then endorse this charter so that everybody is aware of the role of the department and the services it provides. This will be key in future when additional resource or external consultancy is a recommended, in the event of disputes or requirements for material corrective action.

There is no point in wording the compliance charter in regulator speak nor is there any need for people to have studied English language at University before reading your charter. There is always a tendency to use jargon, MBA speak etc. But you'll find if you use the "house" language option the charter will not only be understood better but staff are more likely to accept and recall it.

The charter can of course follow any format you prescribe, however I would suggest you consider including the following;

- a definition of compliance risk

- Overall responsibility for compliance (you may like to include individual responsibility for complying with regulatory requirements etc.)
- The scope and limitations of compliance department, such as the regulators, codes of practice, areas within the department, i.e. financial promotions, complaints etc.
- Any outsourcing or in-sourcing practices when other departments undertake compliance activities
- Any exclusions specific to your department such as legal compliance, financial reporting, health and safety etc.
- the high-level compliance department objectives
    - regulatory framework is in place
    - ethical stance
    - policies and procedures
    - monitoring and management information gathering
    - modus operandi
    - seeking of proactive dialogue with other members of staff
- day-to-day activities at a high level
- powers of the compliance department mentioning oversight
- dealings with the regulator/s
- authority permissions to work with other departments such as;
    - HR
    - legal

- o the board, audit (or other)committee or non-executive directors (if applicable)
- o permission to access any document or record
- o sufficient resources for own use
- o the right to expect cooperation from other departments
- compliance responsibilities for the rest of the firm
    - o notification of complaints or rule breaches
    - o reporting suspicions of money laundering offences
    - o requesting guidance
    - o directing enquiries for regulators through the department
- Performance measurement (how do we know?)
- management information and reporting
- escalation procedures
- approval of the charter
- review of the charter

This should provide you with a workable document that can be flexible enough to grow organically but sufficiently non-prescriptive to be able to interpret it for most events. If you make the charter too detailed, you will be making a rod for your own back

Chapter 7: Mapping Your Territory

There are undoubtedly Compliance Managers in companies across the country that see their daily work as some kind of battle or counter espionage type work which involves sitting in a darkened room rate hours reading rules, interpreting missives, translating guidance or fighting off queries from the operational side of the business. For those people there is little point in understanding or appreciating how your firm fits into the wider regulatory landscape or territory as everything will be a no-can-do.

However if you have a vision of providing the very best compliance service that is possible to your firm each and every day, then you need to understand how and where your firm stands. The first step is identifying the high-level activities explained in the previous chapter however now you must tease out the more detailed aspects and responsibilities of being a Compliance Manager.

This section although vast and sometimes complicated is a fundamental necessity to ensure that the foundations of your compliance department and all the ideas, policies, controls, processes and procedures that you implement are not built on sand. To do this it would be advisable to take a new notebook and cover the following rough sections;

- each entity within your group including appointed reps, introducer appointed representatives or other subsidiary or joint-venture partners that your firm may have entered into business with
- each business unit and support departments within each entity
- external service providers including anything that maybe outsourced from IT to Para-planning, Legal to Banking.

- the regulatory jurisdiction in which you are operating, for most this will be the UK and at most Europe however many firms these days offer offshore investment services
  - Within your jurisdiction you need to identify all of the regulators and any standards or best practice setting, parties that may contain a quasi-regulator status as well as the obvious legislation, regulation and code etc.
- product services and specific business activities across the range from front, middle and back office, as well as any general insurance, mortgages, financial and investment planning
- common documentation used within the businesses across all entities for regulatory matters such as disclosure, financial promotions et cetera and any other relevant areas that may apply in the periphery

You will gather from this exercise that the requirements to be a good Compliance Manager takes you beyond the normal scope of compliance into legal, marketing as well as governance, company secretarial and office management. As it's in your interest to utilise these additional areas from a relationship point of view, it is often best not to approach these with all guns blazing.

In gathering this information and immersing yourself in the knowledge of these other departments you will find that others will be asking you why you need to know how the IT system works, a subordinated loan is treated for the owners or even just how the HR recruitment process works, and you need to be confident in your response that by having even a broad understanding of the firm's involvement will help put your own activities into context and therefore assist you in identifying compliance risks or potential breach areas.

It is all very well understanding financial promotions to the degree that is required by the regulations but if you do not understand the content of the financial promotion, the product or service being offered within that advertisement or script, then simply by applying the rules will do you no service whatsoever. The world is full of unemployed academics.

Additionally, from a relationship point of view, you will gain credibility with the people within these other areas and should take more and more interest in what they do and how they do it. Providing you do not find ways to pick holes in their processes or procedures before you understand how they operate, and conduct a sensible and properly scoped assessment, then your credibility will soar. If, however, you are unable to provide a suitable answer regarding why you need to know, within a reasonable time period you will lose not only their confidence but also any impetus you may have built up. Beware of processes and procedures which are conducted for reasons that are non-regulatory but essential for customer service reasons, which you may be unable to get your head around immediately: just accept it and move on, the time for testing will come later.

I'm not suggesting that you learn everything about each and every department, how the administration system files and stores the elements they are required to keep however you should be able to speak to any staff member with confidence about anything they may be required to do. By having a working knowledge of all departments there is less likelihood anyone will try to pull over your eyes.

These things would be so much easier if we had a one size fits all rulebook segregated into specific business models, however because of the diversity of financial services within not only the UK but also Europe, this is not possible. I will try to give you a simple catch all type of model to capture the information you need in the next chapter.

When you are conducting your data gathering or fact-finding, you sometimes find you experience difficulty obtaining some of the information. There are usually only two reasons for this, and they are;

- the information is not relevant to your business, for example you may not have the background or remit to cover these areas in any shape or form therefore strikeout and continue; or

- The information is not readily available but is relevant to your business, for example you have an outsourced agreement but there seems to be no feedback, management information, or data available regarding their business activities other than level of activity. This obviously needs further investigation after your data gathering exercise, so that you can find what is going on and implement any remedial action necessary.

I cannot reinforce enough that at this stage you should only be data gathering and not forming opinions, criticising, providing solutions or anything else that would jeopardise the overall exercise, your credibility or respect from your peers. Until you understand completely how everything into relates or conversely doesn't interrelate then mapping out your territory so that you can see the bigger picture is a far higher priority than putting out bushfires that may randomly appear.

In the next chapter I will cover the areas of your corporate influence, regulators and other industry bodies, legislative environment and a brief note on financial products and services.

Chapter 8: Rules Mapping

Whilst predominantly dealing with Compliance Manager's responsibilities, we can of course extend this to a general retail distribution channels in principle if not in detail.

With any financial services firm but it is the very first step for the Compliance Manager when identifying the territory that they will be working within to ensure that they have correctly identified all operating entities and the relationship they have with the principle firm. There are of course complexities if you are regulated in another home state and exercising passport rights into the UK, but for the purposes of this book we will deal with UK authorised and regulated firms.

The complexities of financial services companies will become more involved with risk and governance, service and product development, as well as normal business practices of mergers and acquisitions over the lifetime of the business. On initial appointment to the position, or if starting anew for whatever reason, it is important for the Compliance Manager to understand the impact of the following;

- UK branch offices
- Overseas branch or rep offices
- Other UK regulated firms within your own group
- Any UK and regulated firms within your own group (Beware: these may be governed by other requirements or separate regulators.)
- Any special purpose vehicles
- Any investment funds such as distributor influenced funds (*see note below*)
- joint ventures partially owned by other firms
- appointed representative firms

- Any dormant firms where previous liabilities exist.

Your responsibilities for all these firms may not be immediately apparent however is best to keep a log of all such relevant details in case you need the information quickly. Even if you're not responsible for these firms you may still require knowledge of how they interact with your responsibilities to make sure there is no conflict in the future. Sometimes it is sufficient to know that the firm exists and have a contact number and name attached to it as we all know things can change rapidly you may suddenly need to have more information.

***Note**: Distributor-influenced funds are created for the clients of a particular distributor, typically an adviser firm. They could be designed on a bespoke basis for the distributor or they could be set up using an existing fund that is tailored for the distributor. Fund administration and management is outsourced to other firms but the distributor may have a degree of influence over the fund (short of day-to-day asset selection). It may be, for example that the distributor is able to:*

- *influence the hiring (or removal) of the delegated investment manager;*

- *create accountability of the investment adviser by attending investment committees; or;*

- *appoint (or remove) the Authorised Corporate Director*

They are commonly arranged as OEICs (where they may be known as broker OEICs or distributor owned funds) but may also take other structures (like insurance funds). We have chosen to refer to them as distributor-influenced funds in this factsheet, as this term covers the full range of possible structures

Although the list we provide is not exhaustive, it is fairly comprehensive, and should you consider anything else is applicable, please add it accordingly.

Suggested data requirements to complete your role would be as follows;

Company Full name:

Make sure you use the correct corporate designation and note what any abbreviations stand for such as PLC. LLP, SA, PV LTD etc.

Previous name/s

A cursory glance of the FCA register will provide you with numerous companies that were known by previous names. Some longer standing clients or staff may still refer to the old company name or structure, while meaning the new and it is as well for you to be aware of the distinction.

Registered address

Obviously official documents agreements contracts etc. are required to have the registered address.

Place of business address/es

This may be different to the registered office and you will need to know the best place to go to when you doing monitoring visits. Also some firms may have multi-locations and it is important for you to know this in your planning.

Key contact names etc.

When you need to get in touch quickly these details are invaluable. If you record the website address and any e-mail domains used these may be important when you come to consider any financial promotions responsibilities as well as data security and business continuity planning.

Corporate data

Basic data such as place of incorporation, date of incorporation, tax registration number, business registration number or operating licence number (in some jurisdictions) are not critical but very useful to have at your fingertips from time to time.

Local regulator details

There could be more than one regulator so ensure that you note all impacting legislative or regulatory entities.

Regulatory approval dates

These are obvious.

Capitalisation or regulatory capital

This will obviously have an impact on a regulatory resources; the amount of money the firm can lend or borrow, the maximum type or size of transactions that can be undertaken and will obviously factor in the frequency and content of any regulatory reports that may be required either locally or through the principle firm.

Financial year end

The main impact of this will be on financial reporting dates

Owners and other influencing factors

You need to know who within the firm have is a significant influence whether they are executive directors or not. Regulators use the term controllers and define these as those with whom the firm has close links. You should also at this point be aware of the person to whom should be sending you management information and for you to enquire about any local regulation that may require reports from you.

Listing

Is the entity listed on a stock market? There may well be stock market rules to comply with as well.

Subsidiaries, rep offices and branches

There are various rules relating to threshold conditions for authorisation regarding close links and access of the regulator to the supervision of these firms.

Powers of attorney

If these exist you have to understand who the legal authority is that is able to sign on behalf of the entity, who signs the returns to the regulator and obviously who can approve contracts.

Senior management

All senior staff will need regulator approval including significant influence functions and we will deal with the approved person's regime later.

Committees and other official bodies

Company power is often emanating from committees and you need to understand how the compliance elements are impacted by these committees as well as their structure and reporting lines. Terms of reference for each committee is vital not only to identify the composition of the committee but also to clarify their read it.

Compliance Officer and MLRO

These people are going to be your peers and obviously good cooperation with them should be reciprocated as you may need to get hold of them are relatively easily in times of crisis. If they know their business well enough they should be able to provide you with useful advice and support as well as guidance for their specific firm or culture within their jurisdiction. They could sometimes be useful to understand the rest of the senior management roles if they extend beyond the directors and compliance officer.

Internal annex table auditors

If your firm is sufficiently large to have both internal and external auditors then you will need to form a good working relationship with both of these. Obviously internal auditors will be able to complement compliance monitoring and you can annually agree with them a planned approach so that you are not crossing swords unnecessarily. Additionally, if they are an outsourced arrangement, can also, sometimes provide you with a good steer regarding compliance issues that they have come across in other organisations.

Legal advisers and/or other corporate service providers

Often firms will have a favoured link with legal providers or other major service providers. If there are any outsourced agreements these need to be checked against the FCA requirements and ensure that no material functions have been outsourced.

Obviously with very large organisations you could have business units within each entity that may or may not be duplicated and as this is unlikely to be the norm I will ignore this specific area at this time. There is of course a need to understand the business units within your own firm whether these units take the form of sales teams or specialist areas with their own distinct advisers you will obviously need to understand certain basics such as, and in addition to the above ;

- management compliance concerns
- specific product services or activities
- the main activity for income generation
- anything considered as a unique selling point
- any point of sale or post sale documentation used if different to the principal
- target client base or segment
- methods of advertising and marketing
- IT systems
- most valued clients
- top deals of the previous 12 months
- complaints

- challenges
- governance; policies and procedures and how they may differ to the principal
- conflicts of interest, regulatory issues in the last 12 months, risks, regulatory contact the last 12 months
- any major changes in the last 12 months; and
- Any major changes planned for the next 12 months.

At this stage it may also be worth thinking about risk management and mitigation programs to be implemented for each legislative section you may have responsibility for within your firm. You might like to consider covering the broad list below;

- Specific responsibility if the requirement is for anybody other than the compliance officer.
- A gauge or measure in some way of how the firm is impacted by this legislation and specifically the subparts affected.
- What you consider the key risks to be.
- The controls you have identified in relation to each risk.
- Any weaknesses in the control framework that may need to be addressed; these can be risk rated.
- An action plan prepared and designed to address any weaknesses that you may have uncovered in your investigations. You should of course ensure that you record and track progress regularly.
- A review frequency for when you are going to revisit your current findings. More complex areas are likely to need a more frequent visit.
- The overall risk rating you apply to this specific area of legislation and this should take into account the

seriousness of penalties or frequency they are imposed by the regulator.

UK legislation text can easily be found on the Internet and to specific sites that are useful are the UK Statute Law database (www.StatuteLaw.gov.uk) and the Office of Public Sector Information (www.OPSI.gov.uk), although beware the latter as repealed or amended or subsequent legislation is not clearly indicated and the original text can still be found.

The detailed rules mapping

The high-level rules map is going to be fairly similar for all UK regulated firms. Once you start increasing the depth of information you may well find that not all parts of each law will apply to every section of your firm. Whereas it will appear to be a bit of skipping from one relevant law to another, it is also important to realise that your firm has existing policies and procedures in place that may reference out of date legislation these are obviously risk areas for you to address.

If your firm is a small concern with one main line of business then a single regulatory rules map is more likely to be applicable however when you link up to the FCA handbook you will find that not all sections within these sourcebooks will necessarily apply to your firm so you could end up with large gaps or blanks in your matrix.

To construct your matrices correctly there are two methods you can use one being the bottom-up approach, which are self-explanatory insomuch as you start at the activity level and consider all the legislative and regulatory impacts that may apply.

The top-down approach is a more detailed and time-consuming rules mapping exercise where you may be searching for applicability to a certain law which may, not actually apply to your type of business. If you're a large company and operate in diverse fields such as running distributor influenced funds or even a stockbroking facility then the top-down approach may well be more applicable. Although this can be tedious it can also be worthwhile if you have the time.

Typical sample rules map

If you draw yourself a spreadsheet with the column headings referencing the handbooks starting with SYSC, COBS, BIPRU, INSPRU, etc. and with rows complete the titles of functions such as trading desks, middle office, settlement and other areas of activity. For retail distribution it could be, life sales, pensions sales, investment sales, mortgages etc. across the top. Your matrix will soon take shape. From this basic matrix you can identify where the SYSC or COBS handbooks would apply to your firm, and if it is not applicable, perhaps why not.

If you had offices or branches in other jurisdictions this very simple matrix could be replicated for the local regulator or judiciary that may impact it.

Chapter 9: Financial Products and Services

Being a successful Compliance Manager is difficult unless you understand the full range of products and services offered by your firm. Failure to fully understand these would hinder any advice or recommendation that you may be called upon to provide to your colleagues. Additionally of course, there is the possibility that somebody, at some time, may try and pull the wool over your eyes to get a decision approved. Your personal stature and credibility will obviously also suffer if they think you can be easily hoodwinked.

Obviously these days there are an enormous amount of financial services products sold through even the most modest retail distribution offices including all the wraps, platforms or other offering, not to mention the innovative general insurance and mortgage products that are emerging post the credit crisis. A detailed knowledge and understanding of the company's permissions and the appropriate exemptions and/or waivers will obviously assist you greatly.

You should also be aware of all products recently sold in both name and generic type to ensure that an adviser or team are not going off-piste with their recommendations, and to perhaps review the risk rating sample of cases to be checked. Your new business department will not always understand the products sold could be classified as a higher risk than normal and may not understand the anagrams concerned.

Once you've established the product sold and the pattern of sales across the business then it's time to actually start the serious work and check for the latest regulatory stance on anything you are unsure of. This can be done on the regulator's website with the most recent documents produced consultation paper or policy statement.

With the embedding of the Retail Distribution Review well under way, new service offerings will undoubtedly be created to satisfy certain categories or segments of client's service by the business. It's important that you fully understand the level of service being provided and the fees charged. It is more than likely that a transaction only client, whilst understanding they receive no ongoing advice, may need it made clearer to them that they still have the full range of consumer protection to them regarding the suitability of the advice, concerning that transaction.

Alternatively, advisers might opt for an execution only platform to keep wealth clients content for the smaller repeat transactions such as ISAs, so that they are not paying £200 an hour simply to invest further monies into their plans. These transactions, will not normally qualify for financial ombudsman redress or FSCS protection unless the original advice was made by the adviser or their firm. This highlights the need to keep accurate records.

There also has to be a distinction made between products or services that are provided to the clients and that may not be regulated by the FCA or PRA. The services could well be covered by other regulation or legislation such as tax planning, will writing, unsecured loans and debt counselling (although these may now be regulated by the FCA for CCA aspects) or some kinds of corporate advice.

Identifying the products provided by your firm is probably the easiest step, however linked to these products, services or activities are the financial promotions, point-of-sale documentation, post-sale documentation and, of course, the file construction of each client whether paper or electronic to quickly and easily demonstrate provider or regulatory miscellaneous documentation supplied such as for AML purposes etc.

Whilst this obviously has an impact on other documentation within the sales process, it will not be necessary at this time to review all of this associated documentation. The main focus at this time should be of product documentation only.

Regulated activities

Regulated activities are defined as;

(in accordance with section 22 of the Act (Regulated activities)) any of the following activities specified in Part II of the Regulated Activities Order (Specified Activities):

(a) Accepting deposits (article 5);

(aa) issuing electronic money (article 9B);

(b) Effecting contracts of insurance (article 10(1));

(c) Carrying out contracts of insurance (article 10(2));

(d) Dealing in investments as principal (article 14);

(e) Dealing in investments as agent (article 21);

(ea) bidding in emissions auctions (article 24A);

(f) Arranging (bringing about) deals in investments (article 25(1));

(g) Making arrangements with a view to transactions in investments (article 25(2));

(ga) arranging (bringing about) regulated mortgage contracts (article 25A (1));4

(gb) making arrangements with a view to regulated mortgage contracts (article 25A (2));

(gc) arranging (bringing about) a home reversion plan (article 25B (1));

(gd) making arrangements with a view to a home reversion plan (article 25B (2));

(ge) arranging (bringing about) a home purchase plan (article 25C (1));

(gf) making arrangements with a view to a home purchase plan (article 25C (2));

(gg) operating a multilateral trading facility (article 25D);

(gh) arranging (bringing about) a regulated sale and rent back agreement (article 25E (1));

(gi) making arrangements with a view to a regulated sale and rent back agreement (article 25E (2));

(h) Managing investments (article 37);

(ha) assisting in the administration and performance of a contract of insurance (article 39A);

(i) Safeguarding and administering investments (article 40); for the purposes of the permission regime, this is sub-divided into:

(i) Safeguarding and administration of assets (without arranging);

(ii) Arranging safeguarding and administration of assets;

(j) Sending dematerialised instructions (article 45(1));

(k) Causing dematerialised instructions to be sent (article 45(2));

(l) Establishing, operating or winding up a collective investment scheme (article 51(1) (a)); for the purposes of the permission regime, this is sub-divided into:

(i) Establishing, operating or winding up a regulated collective investment scheme;

(ii) Establishing, operating or winding up an unregulated collective investment scheme;

(m) Acting as trustee of an authorised unit trust scheme (article 51(1) (b));

(n) Acting as the depositary or sole director of an open-ended investment company (article 51(1) (c));

(o) Establishing, operating or winding up a stakeholder pension scheme (article 52 (a) 46);

(oa) 44 providing basic advice on stakeholder products44 (article 52B);

(ob) establishing, operating or winding up a personal pension scheme (article 52(b));

(p) Advising on investments (article 53); for the purposes of the permission regime, this is sub-divided into:

(i) Advising on investments (except pension transfers and pension opt-outs);

(ii) Advising on pension transfers and pension opt-outs;

(pa) advising on regulated mortgage contracts (article 53A);

(pb) advising on a home reversion plan (article 53B);

(pc) advising on a home purchase plan (article 53C);

(pd) advising on a regulated sale and rent back agreement (article 53D);

(q) Advising on syndicate participation at Lloyd's (article 56);

(r) Managing the underwriting capacity of a Lloyd's syndicate as a managing agent at Lloyd's (article 57);

(s) Arranging deals in contracts of insurance written at Lloyd's (article 58);

(sa) entering into a regulated mortgage contract (article 61(1));

(sb) administering a regulated mortgage contract (article 61(2));

(sc) entering into a home reversion plan (article 63B (1));

(sd) administering a home reversion plan (article 63B (2));

(se) entering into a home purchase plan (article 63F (1));

(sf) administering a home purchase plan (article 63F (2));

(sg) entering into a regulated sale and rent back agreement (article 63J (1));

(sh) administering a regulated sale and rent back agreement (article 63J (2));

(si) meeting of repayment claims (article 63N (1) (a));

(sj) managing dormant account funds (including the investment of such funds) (article 63N (1) (b));

(t) Entering as provider into a funeral plan contract (article 59);

(u) Agreeing to carry on a regulated activity (article 64); which is carried on by way of business and relates to a specified investment applicable to that activity or, in the case of (l), (m), and (n) and (o), is carried on in relation to property of any kind.

Designated Investments

Designated Investments are classed as;

A security or a contractually-based investment (other than a funeral plan contract and a right to or interest in a funeral plan contract), that is, any of the following investments, specified in Part III of the Regulated Activities Order (Specified Investments), and a long-term care insurance contract which is a pure protection contract:

(a) Life policy (subset of article 75 (Contracts of insurance));

(b) Share (article 76);

(c) Debenture (article 77);

(ca) alternative debenture (article 77A);

(d) Government and public security (article 78);

(e) Warrant (article 79);

(f) Certificate representing certain securities (article 80);

(g) Unit (article 81);

(h) Stakeholder pension scheme (article 82(1)43);

(ha) Personal pension scheme (article 82(2)); 43

(hb) Emissions auction product (article 82A) where it is a financial instrument.

(i) Option (article 83); for the purposes of the permission regime, this is sub-divided into:

(i) Option (excluding a commodity option and an option on a commodity future);

(ii) Commodity option and option on a commodity future;

(j) Future (article 84); for the purposes of the permission regime, this is sub-divided into:

(i) Future (excluding a commodity future and a rolling spot forex contract);

(ii) Commodity future;

(iii) Rolling spot forex contract;

(k) Contract for differences (article 85); for the purposes of the permission regime, this is sub-divided into:

(i) Contract for differences (excluding a spread bet and a rolling spot forex contract);

(ii) Spread bet;

(iii) Rolling spot forex contract;

(l) Rights to or interests in investments in (a) to (k) (article 89) but not including rights to or interests in rights under a long-term care insurance contract which is a pure protection contract.

Retail Investment Products (RIPs)

The "*RETAIL DISTRIBUTION REVIEW (ADVISER CHARGING) INSTRUMENT 2010*" introduced the designation of Retail Investment Products or RIPs whereby these products must be considered (and documented) by independent advisers who may hold themselves out to the market to being independent.

These are;

(a) A life policy; or

(b) A unit; or

(c) A stakeholder pension scheme (including a group stakeholder pension scheme) 113; or

(d) A personal pension scheme (including a group personal pension scheme) 113; or

(e) An interest in an investment trust savings scheme; or

(f) A security in an investment trust; or

(g) any other designated investment which offers exposure to underlying financial assets, in a packaged form which modifies that exposure when compared with a direct holding in the financial asset; or

(h) A structured capital-at-risk product; whether or not any of (a) to (h) are held within an ISA or a CTF.

Chapter 10: Compliance in Support Functions

This is a very brief chapter to cover an obvious area, but one which does need to be mentioned.

Who else within your firm needs to understand the compliance and regulatory requirements? The firm's principles? HR? Legal? The receptionist? File clerks? The answer is obviously that they all do. The main difference will be the level of knowledge required depending on their role and responsibilities within the firm. In fact it would be nigh on impossible to name anybody within the firm that need have no knowledge of compliance or regulatory impact on their employer. This concept needs to be carried forward into areas such as financial crime, because all staff could be exposed to price sensitive or confidential information regarding clients and their affairs.

The sales manager's or principles of the business will obviously need to be as familiar as you are with the compliance requirements that appertain to their specific responsibilities. The Compliance Manager's role requires that you find a way to get them to that level if you find they are lacking in any way, shape or form. This is not only important so that they may support you with a good understanding, but it is also vital for them so they can stand their ground should they be challenged by any of their staff regarding compliance requirements.

Training your staff again falls on the Compliance Manager and they themselves should know what is expected by each department or team and deliver this in a combination of ways whether by policy, online training, presentation, external training company providing a training package, external training courses, workshops and practical sessions perhaps attached to staff meetings, roundtable discussions, regulatory briefing memo circulated as and when or a précis of certain documents promulgated on an ad hoc basis.

Set Plan

- Set up meetings with these other departments
- Check understanding
- Explain where what you can provide
- Explain where you need them to and specific areas of friction
- Agree joint actions
- Cascade lessons down to your staff

Ongoing Training

Once training has been conducted at least initially or on induction, it is often a good practice to have a certain amount of training refresher each year provided to the staff and gain their annual attestation to confirm they are up to date and understand what their requirements are. Specific or specialist training may be available through certain institutes or organisations from the firm's associations and these would normally be for senior management or principles where it would not be cost-effective to run these in-house for such a small number. Do not forget that any part-time or contract workers are required to have full understanding of their obligations and responsibilities and for this you may need to have input from the HR world. Any failings to complete annual refresher training after an agreed period should have a contractual disciplinary process attached. These people are not only risking losing up-to-date knowledge or not being TCF and or breaching Conduct Risk requirements, but they are also letting down the whole firm.

Cause and Effect

With any firm that has grown from humble beginnings there is always a family feeling about it and it is hard to consider that somebody may not share the same values as the rest of the team. This inherent blindness must be overcome by the Compliance

Manager for them to be effective, as any failing to meet your regulatory responsibilities could result in a personal fine as well as regulatory censure or scrutiny of the firm.

In the evolving regulatory world, governance, risk and culture are going to be increasingly put under the microscope by the regulator in an attempt to ensure that companies are being run as businesses rather than financial sales houses. With this brings additional requirements that many senior managers or directors/partners are not totally familiar, and in support of them Management Information (MI) will need to be made more robust and relevant. Let us not forget that senior management are responsible for the corporate governance of the firms in their charge. Corporate governance is an expansive concept but can easily be summed up as "the direction and management of corporate affairs in order to maximise shareholder value."

The principles of the business are ultimately responsible for all of the firm's compliance arrangements and activities are demonstrated in the FSAs (now FCAs) "Dear CEO" letters. Since the expansion of the common platform firm definition for most firms the chapters 4 to 10 of the Systems and Controls Sourcebook (SYSC) will apply (and 11, 12, 18, 19a & 21 may also apply depending on your firm) and need implementation if not already in progress. This means that all senior management should receive full training to the extent and nature of their regulatory responsibilities and should be fully aware of all consequences they may face if they do not meet these responsibilities appropriately.

These responsibilities extend to ensuring the smooth and safe running of all activities within the firm and the impact of any external influences or actions such as,

- apportionment and oversight
- approved persons regime
- Chinese walls (if appropriate)

- insider dealing and sensitive information
- data protection
- confidentiality of both client and staff
- company announcements and press releases
- companies act responsibilities
- outside activities
- board or management meetings
- risk management
- marketing and financial promotions
- capital adequacy and Prudential regulation
- outsourcing
- regulatory fees
- complaints, training and competence etc.

Most firms are likely split into at least two where the front office or customer relationship management occurs and the back office, where the supporting functions for the processing of the work generated by the front office and the general operation of the firm overall is managed. If there are any shortcomings with the levels of understanding or if the culture is not adapting to embrace the regulatory changes, this effect will become evident and is mainly down to one cause, and that is the way you manage these other departments and management. Don't let it happen to you.

Chapter 11: Regular Compliance Activities

As it is assumed that the reader is of at least an intermediate level, and as previously stated, I will not be discussing the mundane regular compliance activities such as regulatory reporting, complaints reporting, client money or other regulatory requirement as these may well change in the future as the regulators evolve with the environment.

Firms are often involved in widely differing styles of business, and the content although broadly similar, may vary considerably from firm to firm. However the Compliance Manager's job will be fairly similar across all types and I will describe some of the best ways of accomplishing these tasks in the rest of this chapter.

Too often these everyday activities which constitute the firm's compliance regime are conducted from a common-sense perspective and often executed as a matter of course. These activities are not rocket science but they are requirements that everybody is aware of and to not conduct them would mean breaching the FSMA as well as internal procedures that you have implemented for your firm to ensure consistency.

These regular processes and procedures that are followed by the Compliance Manager and the compliance team, if there is one, provide the firm with a certain amount of comfort that the controls are not only in place that is tested on a regular basis to ensure the firm is operating compliantly. There is however, as always with these familiar processes, a danger that corners may be cut or indeed whole processes may be bypassed, sometimes with the most innocent of reasons but as we know familiarity breeds contempt and it is important to have a written procedure to refer back to in case you feel the activity is no longer sufficient or conclusive. Heuristics is a particular issue that the FCA has recognised within the Conduct Risk area, and these should be eradicated within your firm.

If you are new to the position of Compliance Manager, then the advice I will provide on the activities you need to consider and document accordingly will prepare you for the closest scrutiny, if carried out correctly. The detail I will provide is of course current when writing this book and I will endeavour to ensure that it remains high level so that revision on your part need only be conducted on major regulatory changes.

So what regular compliance activities do we need to consider?

I will provide you with a selection of topics and accompany it with objectives explanations and actions required and if there is any further information or references then I will apply them accordingly. I will also provide you with a fairly long list of remaining areas future work out for yourself. If you have conducted your rules mapping and legislation mapping exercise from chapter 5 should be quite easy for you. Often while conducting this exercise various other ideas and innovations will spring to mind so please make sure you capture these and take action on them separately.

One of the main focuses for the previous regulator was upon the business risks, culture, controls, and governance of small and medium-sized firms. I am conscious not to spell out in a Janet and John style the full detail of actions that may be required but I will give some salient points for you to grow according to your firm.

Activity: Compliance culture and ethics

Objective

To ensure the corporate culture within your firm consistently promotes ethical business as well as treating customers fairly.

Explanation

There is no point in writing policies or conducting training or even arranging for attendance of external courses if your firm is compliance culture poor. Staff and Appointed Persons will always attempt to find a way around any standards that may be set, and in many cases will ignore them unless they are committed to the compliance culture required of them.

The FSA in recent years moved from a rules-based culture whereby they previously prosecuted offenders under sections from the rulebook and have moved to referring to principles. This has become evident in the final notices issued in the last five years or so and is consistent with adopting a scheme that should take on board the spirit as well as the letter of the sourcebooks.

It should also be remembered that it is in our best interests to act ethically and morally because the industry has suffered enough with too many dodges and scams and if the UK has this reputation internationally the financial services giants may well up sticks and move to other jurisdictions. The recently implemented UK Bribery Act is looked up to by a number of nations across the globe as an innovative and clear-cut piece of legislation which they will no doubt attempt to emulate over time.

Actions

Trying to instil a conscience into a group of people is certainly a challenge and not one that you can write a policy for. Changing a mind-set of any group of people requires an installation of respect and fair play and even transparency toward customers, employees and peers.

Very often this is required to be done by leaders and is set as a tone from the top exercise but the Compliance Manager has the role of acting as an ethical and moral compass, agony aunt and a kind of overseeing corporate conscience being supported by the senior management who will reinforce and recommend the required culture changes at every opportunity.

Quite often the professional institutes will insist on and ethics module as a requirement for the member to achieve a certain status, more so in Chartered Institute, but there are also courses in ethics and financial services commercially available.

Although most firms will have a code of ethics covering not only regulatory issues but also staff behaviour, whistleblowing etc. it may also be worth considering establishing a committee with a focused towards ethics and reputational risk where staff can discuss any plans or changes from a moral perspective and bring to the table any areas of disciplinary or corrective action that may be required, depending on the membership of your committee.

Activity: Compliance manual maintenance

Objective

Although a compliance manual is not a regulatory requirement it is usually a regulatory expectation that one is maintained in some form and provides a point of reference for not only regulatory requirements but also ancillary policies such as data protection, whistleblowing, outsourcing etc. if distinct policies do not exist.

Explanation

This document provides a central resource for staff to refer to for a number of issues. From a regulatory perspective you can spell out what potential penalties could be from non-adherence to things such as anti-money laundering or terrorist financing breaches, failure to adhere to the statements of principles for approved persons or even data security.

Writing a comprehensive compliance manual is a time-consuming job and many firms look to a consultancy or even a law firm to purchase and adapt such a manual. Compliance Consultant sell a generic compliance manual on their website at http://www.complianceconsultant.org.

The compliance manual also provides the Compliance Manager with a level of cover in discharging his responsibilities because if the manual is sufficiently comprehensive and covers the requirements of staff and is made available to those members of staff they will be unable to claim that they had not been told what the rules were.

There are mixed opinions as to whether ancillary policies can be maintained sufficiently within the compliance manual or included as appendices of that document compared to having stand-alone policies which are merely referred to in the compliance manual. At the end of the day this is a personal choice and there are no rules as to which is the most appropriate.

Actions

the basic content of any compliance manual should be what it is and why it is important to be there; a description of the compliance function and the responsibilities of the Compliance Manager including all hats which may include data protection officer, compliance manager etc.; a description of the firm's permissions and any exemptions or specific variations; the relevant requirements applicable to your firm and how they impact staff; how staff can comply with the rules in discharging their duties and the penalties involved if anything was to go wrong; further sources of information or guidance from policies and other manuals internally as well as externally.

Not only when new staff join is the compliance manual required to be read and confirmation of understanding obtained but is also a good idea to implement a process where each member of staff can attest on an annual basis that they've read the compliance manual, understand the content that apply to their position and gained their agreement to comply with the requirements.

Availability of a compliance manual is far easier to maintain these days as you could locate the master copy somewhere on the Internet or cloud service, Windows live is a popular choice for small firms. Locating the document here or on an intranet provides a facility of you giving precise access to staff as well as informing them whenever you update or review the manual depending on what regulatory changes may have occurred. This is obviously far better than maintaining a paper copy in each area, section or department.

It is usually a good practice to include a paragraph in the standard employment contract to require that staff abide by the compliance manual and make them aware that non-compliance or breach of requirements is a disciplinary offence.

Activity: Reviewing policies and procedures

Objective

The policies and procedures are the backbone of the governance of the firm and provide guidance as well as parameters or limitations to staff when performing their duties.

Explanation

There are obviously a number of mandatory policies and procedures documents that firms are required to maintain and these will include such things from the SYSC, PERG, FC and other sourcebooks such as conflict of interest, customer complaints, AML and CTF, whistleblowing, fraud, outsourcing, data security, IT, use access and many others.

Disaster recovery and business continuity should be treated as a very serious and highly important for all staff to not only understand but also practice on an annual basis. For this reason it is imperative that these policies, manuals or guidance notes are kept up-to-date and tested.

As a Compliance Manager you may well come across the situation where a company has grown entrepreneurially and various processes and procedures have grown up with it which may not necessarily be linked up together. It is therefore best practice to identify all of these policies and ensure that they provide a robust and coherent message.

The compliance manual can act as a glue or a central hub to be used as a reference for all these other associated and ancillary policies and the use of it should not be overlooked.

Actions

Obviously you need to identify the areas the FCA require a written policy and your previous study of the sourcebooks will provide this as well as links to other areas that would not only benefit from having a policy, but by doing so will show that you have done your homework and are prepared for the situations contained therein will stop.

You should have a policy approval process in your firm and most documents will need to be approved by the board. These documents should have an internal reference number, a version control number and update information to inform the reader of the changes and when. Whenever a new policy or changed policy occurs you should consider giving the staff affected additional training on the relevant points.

It is often good practice to have an individual responsible for maintaining a policy and that person can ensure that any changes are incorporated in a timely fashion and presented to the board for approval if necessary or at least on an annual basis.

Review of policies should form part of the compliance monitoring plan annually and this can be in any format you should desire.

Activity: Regulatory training

Objective

Simply to ensure that all staff are aware compliance requirements that are applicable to them and where their responsibilities lay.

Explanation

By providing training it not only helps improve the compliance culture by building a relationship with each member of staff but also provides some protection for your position if things go wrong of the staff act inappropriately. If you can demonstrate that these people had initial and regular update training then they cannot claim lack of awareness or employer responsibility.

Even though there may be no formal requirement to train staff or managers or individuals, by not doing so could leave yourself open to criticism and dissent.

Actions

Identify all areas in which training is required or mandate three basis such as anti-money laundering requirements and all other areas where you consider training may be advisable such as handling subject access request under the data protection act. There could be a number of other areas that provide you with concern and you feel training could be advisable and these may be;

- requests from other departments managers
- alterations to your firm's permissions and possibly compliance requirements
- internal or external audit reports
- compliance monitoring plan reports on control weaknesses
- externally reported regulatory action against other firms that you may wish to highlight
- regular press coverage or regulatory hotspots on specific product groups sold
- When you have identified an area in which you need to provide training you need to consider the best time and method of delivery. This could include such activities as;
- inviting an external company to provide training
- inviting a product provider to provide training
- online training and testing
- sending regular regulatory updates or bulletins to staff by e-mail

- running workshops or open sessions at the end of specific meetings
- despatching staff to external courses
- formal presentations made by yourself
- specific documentation that you require reading using a round robin system
- senior management should provide support for your training
- ensure you liaise with HR to enable you to train or brief all workers including temporary or contract depending on the roles fulfilled
- ensure you accurately record the attendees of your training measures and that they are accredited with their attendance accordingly. This therefore means that you follow up with anybody who fails to show and persistent absentees are reported to senior management.

Whereas I have provided you with a reasonable detail in both explanations and action points above there are a number of other activities which you may like to give the same attention to, and these are;

- remedial action plans for weaknesses or regulatory breach
- internal relations within the firm
- compiling the annual compliance monitoring plan
- reviewing and maintaining the compliance contract
- precise requirement of annual attestation
- maintaining a compliance and regulatory risks register
- any advisory and project work including IT
- records of dealings with regulators or official bodies
- preparation for regulatory visits

- relationships with external regulatory consultancies and service providers
- the firm's response to consultation papers
- review rules mapping and legislative or regulatory developments
- regulatory reporting requirements
- ad hoc reporting to the regulator
- membership of professional fees and payment of FCA fees
- keeping the firm up to date with regulatory developments
- passporting
- regulatory agreements and documentation including point of sale
- conflicts of interest
- Conduct Risk
- market abuse and insider trading, including personal account dealing
- disciplinary procedures
- sanctions and watch-list checking
- gifts and entertainment or other inducements
- financial promotions
- whistleblowing
- complaints handling
- rule breach procedures
- approved persons regime
- approval of non-standard advice process

- data protection compliance
- training and competence management
- record-keeping
- new offices, joint ventures and outsourcing
- client categorisation
- management information
- fraud and bribery
- KYC and AML processes including third-party introductions
- PEPs and counterterrorist funding
- MLRO reporting and suspicious activity reports

I'm sure that some of these categories of compliance areas may be able to be merged depending on the size of your firm or the size that you intend your firm to be in the next 2 to 3 years. However from this brief and not totally conclusive list you will see that there are a number of areas to keep your focus. These aspects of compliance monitoring should be broken down into the annual plan and tested at least annually. This is an area where you may sometimes need external assistance from Compliance Consultant and a fresh set of eyes to look at what you may have achieved over recent times.

Chapter 12: Compliance Advisory Work

You may consider that with all the previous chapters' activity you won't have time for any other compliance work however as we all know this never works that way in reality. Whenever we involve other people in regulatory processes, and there is a risk that they may not fully understand, we should always provide an open door for them to enquire or bounce ideas around in preference to the alternative which can lead to breaches and worse.

Compliance advisory work is acting as a font of knowledge, agony aunt, parent and mentor at the same time. I encourage all the Compliance Managers to operate an advice log whereby they record the enquiry method, person, specific area, specific query, rules impacted, response, time taken, any specific conditions and hyperlinks to correspondence. This helps provide a consistency in response as well as a justification of your advice and any references used in evidence. By keeping a record of time taken you can also provide a response to any comments about the level of activity within the compliance department.

Now when considering compliance advisory work I can obviously not provide you with guidance on every query you're likely to encounter. Further to this your response will depend on your own experiences and qualifications however what I hope to achieve is to provide you with some kind of framework and some pointers to deal with issues that will either seem simple and obvious but have further ramifications or maybe appear so complex that you start having visions of screens full of regulatory speak just to provide a yes or no answer.

This process has four stages and these are;
- Obtain as much detail as possible about the query including all the facts relevant to the bringing about of the question.

- Understand everything that you have been presented with and if there are any grey areas clarify them before moving forward.
- When you have a thorough understanding of the query and the requirements of the request, you can then proceed to determine the regulatory impacts of any decision
- Having assessed all of the possible responses, selecting your final response with any requirements, caveats or demands and escalate if further authority is required.

I would challenge anybody who claims to be so thoroughly experienced they will understand every single aspect of what may be asked of them in the future. As a Compliance Manager you not only need to know the regulatory impact but also the corporate impact, company secretary and the applicable law and where to look for any foreign or obscure legislation. It is vital therefore that you should never feel pressured into providing a quick answer until you've been able to consider all of the options and fully understand the query. An incorrect answer could lead to a rule breach but if you say no to something you don't fully understand you could be preventing a perfectly legitimate transaction taking place and therefore the business would lose turnover.

"I KEEP six honest serving-men

(They taught me all I knew);

Their names are What and Why and When

And How and Where and Who.

I send them over land and sea,

I send them east and west;

But after they have worked for me,

I give them all a rest.

I let them rest from nine till five,

For I am busy then,
As well as breakfast, lunch, and tea,
For they are hungry men.
But different folk have different views;
I know a person small—
She keeps ten million serving-men,
Who get no rest at all!
She sends 'em abroad on her own affairs,
From the second she opens her eyes—
One million How's, two million Where's,
And seven million Whys!"

Rudyard Kipling

Kipling had five honest servants named who, what, why, when and where, that he swore kept him on the straight and narrow. I would thoroughly recommend using the same methodology to ensure that you fully understand any requirement made of you and you may find the following worthwhile.

What

What exactly does the query require?
- New service?
- Which products are involved?
- What legislation is involved?

Why

Why is there a query?
- What has happened to bring about this query?
- Why is the previous process or procedure now inadequate?

- Why is it important for this query to be answered?

When

What timescale are we dealing with?
- When is the change scheduled or has it already happens?
- Has there already been an event which you have not been told about? If yes when?
- Is timing important (tax, end of trading year, new legislation etc.)?

How

How will the outcome affect your firm?
- Will there be policy changes required?
- Will the sales process be affected?
- How will this be promulgated?
- How can this be made to work aligned with current processes?

Who

Within your firm is involved with the query?
- What type of client is involved?
- Which regulator may be involved?
- Are there any third parties involved?

Where

Which jurisdiction will this fall under?
- Where are the clients based (residence and domicile)?
- Where do any joint venture or other third party persons fitting?
- Where is the final decision going to impact your firm?
- Where will the process be most effective or used practically?

It is good practice to ask the person using the query to put this in writing by either e-mail or memo as this will give you some time in planning your response with additionally give you a written record for your audit trail. We provide all our clients with an advice log which records all incoming enquiries, person concerned, date, the person who deals with it, the actual response, and hyperlinks to documentation or e-mails for four main reasons;

- You need an audit trail to justify the fact that the query was dealt with and in what timescale according to your charter
- It provides you with a reference for similar enquiries in the future to enable you to be consistent
- It provides an indication of commonly asked questions which in itself will point you in the direction of compliance training needs
- The log also provide you with evidence of the level of enquiries from the business in case you are ever challenged regarding the cost of compliance

Overall, the point I'm trying to make here is that you need to be satisfied and comfortable that you have all the information you need to make the relevant and accurate response. There is nothing more soul destroying or character damaging than responding to a compliance query, half cocked.

With any query you should not feel uncomfortable in going back to the person originating the issue or indeed that person's manager or even subordinates. You can also approach other members of the compliance department or senior managers as in larger organisations some individuals like to play-off one member against another. There may be occasions where you need to ask compliance colleagues in another firm or other departments within your own firm or should you be fortunate enough to have industry association contacts you can of course approach them.

When responding to the enquiries you will of course need to make sure that you have checked all the definitions and glossary, rules and requirements in the area that you are being queried on and it is often as well to check the situation against alternate contexts.

Occasionally drawing the problem out and the exemptions, exceptions and commonalities may also help you decide the best and most straightforward approach in providing your response. For referencing you can obviously use the Oxford English dictionary, Google and your own internal procedures manuals or policy documents if there are risks of conflicts or breaches.

There are obviously specific areas to consider depending on the query, and these are usually broken down into new situations being proposed or situations that have already occurred where a retrospective check is being conducted by the affected persons, auditors or the compliance department. I do not intend to list the potential situations as these will vary depending on your firm; the list will not be exhaustive.

A good list for you to consider incorporating in your advice log categorisation may include;

- regulatory approval
- staff authorisation
- threshold conditions
- fitness and propriety
- complaints
- conduct risk
- breaches
- money-laundering
- conflicts of interest
- fraud

- outsourcing
- rules and guidance
- data security
- technology
- operational losses
- regulatory reporting
- regulatory notifications
- regulatory capital
- acquisitions
- client assets
- business continuity and disaster recovery
- documentation
- regulatory sanctions
- financial promotions (see also separate log)
- policies and procedures
- general enquiries

Following your response and subsequent investigation into the background of the query, you may find that you are not comfortable with the way this was brought about. There may well be a shortfall in your planning, or the company policies may be out of date or require review. So there will remain the questions that you as the Compliance Manager will need to ask yourself concerning;

Policies and procedures: perhaps new policies or procedures may be required to prevent this issue from arising again in which case you will need to identify the owner of that particular process and discuss revision or publication.

Disciplinary: is there a requirement for disciplinary action and if so you may need to engage with HR to ensure the best way to proceed.

Notifications: there may be other persons, regulators or internal management that may need to be advised of the situation in a timely fashion.

Outsourcing: has the outsourcing agreement failed and the required notifications been overlooked mislaid or ignored and you are left to pick up the pieces? Do you need to consider instigating your exit strategy and finding a more reliable provider of your service?

Disaster recovery and business continuity planning: is the situation such that the DR & BCP needs to be invoked? Has the issue or your response required a review of the DR & BCP planning?

Training and competence: has the situation provided you with doubts regarding a member's competence or a training need? Is there an area in which you or your department need further training will refresher training?

Governance: is this situation or issue a repetition of a series of other similar issues which may require a committee or forum to be formed to discuss the best way to deal with future issues?

Internal procedures: if you are being approached for similar issues on a regular basis it may well pay you to construct a framework or template for these types of enquiries and circulate them amongst the staff. A familiar format will assist your investigation and help you provide a response accordingly.

You may very well feel overwhelmed in considering the points that I've raised in this chapter but I think you'll agree they are all relevant and noteworthy. At the end of the day working as the Compliance Manager and having some experience in both the business and compliance I would expect you to initially rely on some basic criteria such as does it pass the smell test? Would you like to see it on the front page of the Financial Times? Is it the kind of issue that you would not only be embarrassed about people knowing you were considering it but would also be difficult to explain to the regulator? And perhaps from a bigger perspective if everybody in your industry sector were to adopt this issue or practice would this have a positive or negative impact on the financial services industry?

Whatever methodology you may use in asking yourself and others the right questions you should be confident enough to stick to your guns and be prepared to hear the answers, whether you like the sound of them or not. Some issues may not be able to be resolved within your firm and may form part of a bigger issue throughout the industry in which case you have three options: undo;

- Approach your trade body to see if others have the same issue
- approach the regulator directly through their helpline
- Park the issue and consider using it as part of a response to a consultation paper when it's appropriate

In summary compliance advisory work can be very demanding, time-consuming, frustrating and sometimes lead to dead ends. However the work can also be very rewarding, informative and educational and is part of ensuring that the Compliance Manager keeps abreast of not only the latest developments but also the changing trends in sales in the financial services industry.

Chapter 13: Compliance with the FCA

We would all like to think that our firm is run not only compliantly the life well-oiled machines. We do of course understand that things sometimes go awry and being able to identify or no the things that are most likely to go wrong gives us huge potential to address situations before they arise.

As with Monty Python's flying Circus quote "nobody expects the Spanish Inquisition", sadly most Compliance Managers and firm's executives do not expect any regulatory investigation. The benefits of understanding the possibilities and process of regulatory all legal scrutiny is an essential tool of the Compliance Manager as when the worst happens you will be called to explain not only the process, assess the damage and provide realistic outcomes for the company.

Personal awareness of the route followed by regulators provides you with a workflow pathway to enable you to prioritise and section work appropriately if some cowboy within your firm has decided that they know better. Although being aware of these processes is a valuable tool by no means should they be used as threats within the firm as your credibility will nosedive, crash and burn.

As we mentioned previously there are obviously several regulatory regimes in the UK and even though we now have the PRA and the FCA, the majority of breaches are likely to be conduct risk related and dealt with primarily by the FCA. Therefore we shall refer only to the FCA as it is the most important to most Compliance Managers as well as being responsible for 90% of compliance activity within the regulated sales arena. Should you operate in alternate jurisdictions or be dual regulated then you will obviously have two understand your own regulators enforcement regime as well as that of the FCA but for most UK compliance persons the FCA rules will apply.

As with any regulator there has to be some method of monitoring, testing, remedying and rectifying any firm's that may infringe the rules and guidance or, as in the case of the FCA, infringement of its statutory and operational objectives. Inappropriate behaviour will be dealt with by the enforcement department which is set up to;

- deter poor conduct
- provide clear corrective remedial action
- penalise bad behaviour
- provide a method of compensation to victims
- promote high standards of competent behaviour

The FCA and PRA derive their powers from the FSMA which provides broad disciplinary authority and the right for both civil and criminal actions to be taken against firms or individuals whether they are regulated by the FCA or not. The FCA does not make the rules and must comply with procedural requirements as well as other legislation such as the proceeds of crime act, human rights act 1998 etc.

Actions by the FCA must be proportionate and fair as well as transparent and these are overseen by the Upper Tribunal.

Conduct Risk

Conduct Risk is the buzz phrase in the financial services world today and jobs abound for "Conduct Risk Managers" or "Head of Conduct Risk"; but very few seem to know what this involves precisely.

There is obviously a great deal of information available including reasons for failure and fines that point you in the right direction, however, try to enter a Boolean search (containing the search term in inverted commas) for "*Conduct Risk*" into the handbook search box and you will find that it is not specifically defined in the regulator's handbook and nothing can be found between "*COND*" and "*conflicts of interest policy*" in the Glossary.

From our experience in designing and implementing these risk frameworks, gleaning what we can from the various speeches and publications, a number of focus areas become evident and include;

- Aligning business models to fair treatment of customers
- Complaints handling
- Product development and governance
- Product Intervention
- Remuneration and reward policies
- Financial Promotion withdrawal and prohibition
- Conflicts of interest
- Incentives
- Wholesale
- Business Continuity

Conduct risk is not new and stems from not only the scandals and mis-selling debacles but is rooted in the Treating Customers Fairly (TCF) initiatives and the rules in COBS. It would appear that the definition of the term is excluded on purpose to make it a reflective and subjective term defined by each company.

Added to this is the complexity of RDR becoming effective from 31 December 2012 and this made significant changes to, and impacted the business models within the investment advice market. Add to this the additional work of implementing MIFID II as well as new regulator with a more intrusive supervisory stance and there are bound to be a great deal of elements that firms are unaware of and will undoubtedly get caught out whenever they are visited or complete "online" or "telephone" assessments.

Conduct Risk is not only an issue here in the UK, but is also a red hot topic for many international regulators as well.

So how do you prove "Conduct Risk" to a satisfactory level?

Firstly you have to understand where conduct risk falls within your own organisation and, in conjunction with the FCA Risk Outlook 2013 and onward, create an idea of where your risks may lie.

The majority of these risks can fall under the Operational Risk umbrella, which a few consultancies can assist you with. You don't necessarily need expensive software for most modest size of firm, but you need to know how you arrive at the findings, and more importantly what you do about them. If you look in the handbook SYSC, you will see that Operational Risk would seem to apply to insurers (SYSC 13) and it could be easy to overlook SYSC 7. SYSC 7.1.2 R states "A common platform firm must establish, implement and maintain adequate risk management policies and procedures, including effective procedures for risk assessment, which identify the risks relating to the firm's activities, processes and systems, and where appropriate, set the level of risk tolerated by the firm." This effectively means that all risks apply to every firm; the three types are Credit Risk, Business or Market Risk and Operational Risk.

Operational Risk is widely accepted to be the Basel II definition that states that operational risk is "the risk of loss resulting from inadequate or failed internal processes, people and systems, or from external events."

Identifying them is only the start as you then have to agree how best to measure them, which creates a real challenge and considerable work for most firms who do not normally deal in this area. Within the three main areas of conduct risk impact; Inherent, Structures & Behaviours and Environmental, there are a great deal of areas that can be measured. Within the first two areas a degree of qualitative and quantitative data already exists, but much of it is overlooked or unreported in most firms.

A Conduct Risk Framework will help in identifying the elements and areas impacted. From this adequate and proportionate measurements can be made for reporting. Overlaid with a rationally decided appetite the data can provide an exception report for Senior Management to consider.

The three phases of good management are definition and measurement, management followed by activity. Running any business is typically conducted this way but the skill of management is actually created and enhanced as a result or product of the activity, therefore there is no definitive answer on how best to manage. The key to these phases is providing accurate and usable data to the second phase. Unfortunately many people when defining the Management Information do this the wrong way round.

Summary

Conduct Risk is not only here to stay as an extension of the TCF Outcomes, but is also going to ramp up as the FCA get a deeper and fuller understanding of what is missing in the retail distribution world. Focussing on your exposure and level of risk is critical to your firm's survival and escaping close regulatory scrutiny, supervision or worse.

The FCA's general enforcement powers

Under the Financial Services and Markets Act 2000 (FSMA), we have an extensive range of disciplinary, criminal and civil powers to take action against regulated and non-regulated firms and individuals who are failing or have failed to meet the standards we require.

Examples of their powers include being able to:
- withdraw a firm's authorisation;
- prohibit an individual from operating in financial services;
- prevent an individual from undertaking specific regulated activities;
- suspend a firm for up to 12 months from undertaking specific regulated activities;

- suspend an individual for up to two years from undertaking specific controlled functions;
- censure firms and individuals through public statements;
- impose financial penalties;
- seek injunctions;
- apply to court to freeze assets;
- seek restitution orders; and
- prosecute firms and individuals who undertake regulated activities without authorisation.

All of this is no doubt riveting reading but what we will deal with in this chapter are;

- identifying the means the regulator has in discovering your secrets
- identify the regulator's hot buttons
- what the regulator can do to find out more about your secrets
- the avenues available to you should you be subject to scrutiny
- possible outcomes if your firm or someone edit is guilty of misconduct

In Chapter 14 we will discuss assessing risk from compliance perspective. In Chapter 15 we will discuss the preparation for a regulatory visit.

Information, information, information

The FCA has numerous reporting requirements from firms and has access to a number of other public records including HMRC returns, companies house reports and with all this information provided on a regular basis it built up a profile of the risk your firm poses towards statutory objectives. Increasingly the use of social media monitoring is providing not only the regulators but also law enforcement agencies a way to monitor illegal promotions, misleading statements or other damaging broadcasts.

There are a number of regular reporting and notification requirements which the FCA uses in its war against misdemeanours. These are typically;

Auditors' reports: each regulated firm must have an appropriate auditor which must be granted adequate access to its records and the FCA takes this auditors role very seriously. It is a criminal offence under section 346 of FSMA to provide false or misleading information to an auditor. The auditor's main duty is to supply three key submissions to the FCA which are; the audit report concerning the firm's regulatory reporting activities; the internal controls letter which comments on the firm's internal controls; the client assets report if applicable.

Application to vary Part IV permissions: requests for a VOP may incur scrutiny if during the approval process they are alerted to the potential that you may have already been acting without the permission.

Rule waiver request: submission of a request to waive or modify a rule may also alert the FCA to an area of your firm's conduct that it may question.

Directly contacting of the FCA for advice: without trying to make you paranoid there is obviously the risk of alerting the FCA to an area they may consider requires further investigation if you approach them about a specific issue. This should not deter you from contacting them if you fail to establish a satisfactory response or answer to a query or situation has arisen.

ONA reporting: a lot of information can be gleaned from the various forms submitted in relation to approved persons such as if you dismiss somebody for gross misconduct, the FCA may turn the tables and wish to investigate if this was due to a lack of controls or procedures within your firm. Another area would be request for someone to be approved conduct and activity for which permissions have not been granted which may mean you are operating illegally. Similar to this reporting regarding appointed representatives can also let the cat out of the bag.

Regulatory reporting requirements: such as;
- Capital adequacy
- Appointed reps/approved persons (as mentioned)
- List of overseas regulators for the group

Controller or close link reporting: a great interest is shown in the controllers of any firm and the close links they may have. If your firm has dealings with or is linked to a disreputable firm in anyway (typically by referral) then you may receive a phone call or visit to discuss the degree of involvement.

Miscellaneous notifications: please form the remainder of the notification requirements such as;
- suspicions of market abuse
- intention to establish a new branch
- material rule breach
- entering into material outsourcing arrangements
- or even evidence of fraud detected

Not only does the FCA use the periodic reporting to provide it with potential areas of conflict, mismanagement or malpractice, but it also has the authority to conduct monitoring visits of any firm that it regulates. These visits can be unplanned or impromptu, but I usually planned giving the firm sufficient warning about the people it may wish to interview and the documentation wish to review beforehand. The FCA must also contractually have similar access to any firm supplier or outsourcer. See chapter 14 for regulatory visit preparation.

Mystery shopping

The FCA may call or visit your firm in an undisclosed manner to ascertain that the standards of advice, suitability and recommendations can be assessed along with the documented sales process that you have. Retail firms were obviously key recipients of visits of this nature.

Other regulatory bodies

In the course of their duties the FCA expects to cooperate with other regulators not only within EU but in fact worldwide. If one or more of these regulators contact the FCA regarding your firm's activities in their jurisdiction there could be good grounds for particular scrutiny. This obviously would be more pertinent to international groups however firm should also be aware of the mislead passport thing rules and if they operate in foreign jurisdictions, that they do not breach the local data protection or other consumer legislation.

There are of course other ad hoc methods of the FCA identifying activities of your firm such as newspaper or press articles, TV or radio programmes that you or colleagues within the firm may appear and questions would be due regarding why it had not received appropriate notice. Financial promotions that appear in the media coupled with complaints and comments submitted to the Advertising Standards Authority (ASA) as well as encouragement for members of the public to contact them on their financial promotions hotline number regarding any breaches or misleading statements within the promotions. Whistleblowing is an obvious area that will raise the FCA's eyebrows as they have a duty to declare their interest followed by an investigation under the Public Interest Disclosure Act 1998 (PIDA) and you will be made aware of such a report fairly quickly. Investigation of other firms or complaint by other firms may implicate your firm or your approved persons personally and a request for an explanation will soon follow.

Hot buttons

You imagine that all and every breach that occurred under the rules and guidelines would be treated with the utmost seriousness. In this a risk-based world of the financial services industry the need to treat each breach equally is removed and ways against the impact of the issue compared to the FCA's statutory or operational objectives. This risk-based methodology is explained further in chapter 14.

The FCA run a business and obviously have to allocate resource according to need. When deciding how seriously the breach affects the statutory objectives there are a number of questions they need to ask of the issue;

Has there been a breach of the rules? This has to be asked to consider if the activity is relevant to any legislation pertinent to the issue not just the FSMA.

Questions to be asked are typically;
- Was there an intention to breach the rule?
- Is this a repeated occurrence for a one-off? Is it likely to re-occur and if so what is the likely frequency?
- How long ago did it take place?
- Was the incident premeditated? Did the firm act recklessly?
- How well does the firm understand the consequences?
- Has there been a breach of the code of practice for approved persons?
- How cooperative has the firm being with the FCA?
- Did the firm notify the FCA immediately it was made aware of the issue?
- Has any customer detriment occurred due to the actions of the firm or its individual?

- Is there any evidence of financial crime occurring?
- Are there likely to be any other retail customers affected?
- Has a remedial action plan been suggested by the firm?
- Is there adequate or appropriate internal controls to prevent this issue of recurring?
- Is this an infringement on Conduct Risk Policy?
- What is the previous record of the firm or individual?
- Has there been a breach of a probation order?
- The false or misleading information provided to the FCA in an attempt to cover up the incident?
- Is there any evidence of negligence by the firm's senior management?

And a whole host of other questions may be asked depending on the circumstances. These all form part of the financial penalty assessment that can be found in the FCA's Decision Procedure and Penalties Manual (DEPP).

Tell me more

The stick has been firmly placed in the hornets' nest and your firm is seen to be waggling it frantically. The FCA needs to know more and is quite happy to use the powers afforded to it or to work in conjunction with other regulatory authorities such as the Serious Fraud Office (SFO), the Crown Prosecution Service (CPS) or the Crown office.

Initially the FCA is likely to simply call a firm on the telephone and request to information about the matter that is of particular interest in an informal way and may request certain records to be transmitted to them and will normally impose a time limit for this to be done. If satisfaction is achieved this point the FCA will conclude their enquiries and nothing more work. However should they need to get tough for any number of reasons, the FCA has the right to demand access to certain information within a specified timeframe even if you do not wish to share it with them

Interviews

The regulator has always been able to ask people to attend interviews on a voluntary basis but they can also compel them to be interviewed which will often be recorded and the subject may be given a recorded interview under caution then the Police and Criminal Evidence (PACE) code will apply to ensure the right balance is struck between rights and freedoms of the individual.

Formal investigations

If the picture is still unclear to the FCA or it appears more like a jigsaw pieces missing they can mount a formal investigation with its own staff or they may appoint other people to investigate on its behalf. The most prevalent of these actions are the skilled person's report under section 166 of FSMA where the firm is invited to appoint an approved skilled person to produce a report within the scope of the requirements notice issued by the FCA on the firm's activities.

Search and seizure powers

The FCA has the ability to request a search warrant permitting the seizure of documents and other information if it suspects there is a risk of tampering or destruction of documents within a firm. They may also use this power if they consider that certain documents or records that are being held may not be available by any other means.

So your name is in the frame

Finding yourself subject to FCA investigation is not a pleasant emotion to experience however the key to dealing with the FCA specifically is to remember Principle 11, "A firm must deal with its regulators in an open and cooperative way, and must disclose to the FCA appropriately anything relating to the firm of which the FCA would reasonably expect notice." Destruction of any evidence, record or documentation of any sort is totally advisable. Deleting data from your computer's hard drive is also not considered to be in your best interests. The worst thing you can do is to try and outsmart the FCA as this will only serve to antagonise and frustrate them. If you have made an error of judgement, inadvertently breached a condition or rule then as usual, honesty is the best policy. It may not do your ego a lot of good but it will maintain your integrity in the eyes of your regulator.

There are certain things you can do to assist your particular case and these are;

Obtain professional assistance

This would include lawyers, accountants and compliance consultants like Compliance Consultant who by definition are likely to know more about the FCA's enforcement process than you do and will have experience in dealing with official requests and interpreting their direction. Do not be under any illusion that the services will be free, they will cost you money but they could keep you in business.

Personal representation

On initial notification from the FCA that they intend to take disciplinary action against you, you can make a representation in support of your own case either written or orally on your own behalf. It is normally accepted to do this within a specific timeframe and the FCA's notice will indicate the current acceptable period.

Financial Services and Markets Tribunal (FSMT)

The FSMT was established to ensure that the FCA disciplinary decisions were subject to independent review. Although established under section 132 of FSMA the FSMT is independent from the FCA and certain matters can be referred to them including removal of approved person status and disciplinary actions against regulated firms. There have been cases where the

tribunal has ruled against the FCA however be very careful if you decide to go down this route as the FSMT can increase any fees or costs which may total more than any fine imposed. The Tribunal can;
- support the initial FCA decision;
- require the FCA not to take the action it proposed in the decision notice;
- require the FCA to take different actions to those set out in the decision
- notice; or
- make recommendations concerning the FCA's rules and procedures

The media

If you feel as though you are really treated poorly by the FCA you can approach the press in the hope that they may take up your case. There are no guarantees and this should be considered as a final option. The press are fickle in what they interpret public interest to me at the best of times.

Publicity and enforcement cases

The FCA will not normally comment on whether we are investigating an issue. They may if appropriate publish information about certain Warning Notices, having first consulted the person to whom the notice is issued. However, they are required to make information public, if appropriate, when they issue a Decision or Final Notice.

The FCA and mediation

The mediation process involves a neutral mediator helping parties to negotiate a settlement. The mediator will not offer an evaluation of each party's case, but will purely assist the negotiation.

If the parties consent, mediation may take place at any stage of the enforcement process. However, mediation is unlikely to be appropriate in cases where the regulator is contemplating bringing a criminal prosecution, or where they need to take urgent action. 6

Trade association

You could try contacting your trade association to see if they will assist you in your case as it may impact other firms within their membership.

Legal Routes

There are also other legal options available to you and seeking advice from a professional is highly recommended in these instances.

So what Can They Do to You?

The more serious courses of action that the FCA may take are set out in their Decision Procedure and Penalties Manual (DEPP) and covers the simple operation of publishing a notice about disciplinary action that it may intend to take, subsequently takes and the date it will take effect.

Anybody facing potential disciplinary action from the FCA will experience the following process (please note this does not cover the bringing of criminal prosecutions or civil proceedings);

Stage one

Investigators appointed. Notice of appointment of investigators are sent the persons concerned that the FCA's discretion.

Stage two

Scope of the investigation in forming the relevant persons of what will be involved including the process, documents and people involved.

Stage three

Work commences by the investigating team reviewing documents taking witness interviews etc. Normally the FCA will undertake an independent legal review internally of the case material.

Stage four

Preliminary Investigation Report (PIR) is provided to the person being investigated and normally 28 days are allocated for a response although an additional time may be requested.

Stage five

Case taken to the Regulatory Decisions Committee (RDC) if the investigation team think this is appropriate. The RDC reviews the report and takes into account any responses to the PIR.

Stage six

If appropriate the RDC sends a warning notice to the person being investigated which will usually deal the further action to be taken. A further 28 days to respond with the potential of requesting extra time is normally available.

Stage seven

If the person concerned wishes to make a representation after receipt of the warning notice the RDC will meet again to consider the new information.

Stage eight

The RDC makes their final decision and will, if appropriate, issue a decision notice. Again there are 28 days available in which to refer the matter to the FSMT. Should the RDC consider there is no case to answer a notice of discontinuance will be issued.

Stage nine

The FCA will publish a final notice and make all details pertinent to the case public and available on their website.

The FCA may in their absolute discretion decide to close down an investigation at any time with the issuance of a private warning or through settlement discussions or by deciding that there are no grounds for enforcement action that are likely to proceed.

The FCA and settlement

Settlement is possible at any stage of the enforcement process.

The Settlement Decision Makers will be drawn from a pool of FCA Directors and Heads of Department. The Settlement Decision Makers will be the ultimate decision makers in any settlement negotiations between Enforcement and a firm or individual. This means all settlement communications are made without prejudice to the Regulatory Decisions Committee (RDC), the FCA decision maker in non-settled cases. Consequently, if the settlement negotiations break down and the case proceeds through a contested administrative process through the RDC, it will not be told about any admissions or concessions made during settlement talks.

It is important to appreciate that 'settlement' in the regulatory context is not the same as settlement of a commercial dispute. An FCA settlement is a regulatory decision taken by the FCA, the terms of which are accepted by the firm or individual concerned. So the FCA must have careful regard to their statutory and operational objectives when agreeing the terms of a settlement.

The FCA operates a discount scheme for financial penalties (and/or in relation to periods of suspension) on early settlement. In outline, this operates as follows: if settlement is reached, the FCA and the person concerned will agree in principle the amount of a financial penalty, taking into account all the factors set out in the Decision Procedure and Penalties manual (apart from the existence of the discount scheme itself). A discount will be applied to this amount, depending on when settlement is reached as follows:

Stage 1 (early settlement stage): 30%

Stage 2 (up to the expiry of the period for making written representations to the RDC): 20%

Stage 3 (up to the issue of the Decision Notice): 10%

Other Potential Outcomes

Although the enforcement process detailed above can be entered into there are other potential outcomes other than the no action option. These come in many guises as the range of powers under FSMA are considerable and provide the FCA with a number of discretionary options.

Potential outcomes for you could be (in the best reverse order);
- Informal requirement to change or keep the FCA informed about developments
- Individual guidance which may clarify the interpretation of rules
- Variance of permissions at the FCA's initiative
- Cancellation of a permission
- Cancellation of part IV permissions entirely
- Injunctions in connection with UNFCOG, freeze assets, restrain or remedy a course of conduct
- Withdrawal of approved person status
- Prohibition of individuals preventing them from undertaking, working or carrying out particular activities
- Restitution, redress and compensation
- Insolvency orders
- Public censure
- Fine

- FCA prosecution
- FCA caution
- Private warning
- Notification to and assistance of an authority other than the FCA
- Action by an authority other than the FCA
- Action for damages
- Unenforceability of agreements
- Referral to non-FCA related complaints scheme
- damage to corporate and personal reputation
- breach of employment contract
- strategic closure of firm

A review of the FCA's website and their "latest publications" section will provide you with innumerable opportunities to see final notices issued against individuals and firms detailing their offence, misconduct, rule breaches or principal infringements, reason for fine and or censure and whether or not they referred to the FSMA. Keeping a list of these and reminding your firm on occasions of the offences incurred may help dissuade your colleagues from being tempted to ignore the compliance rules.

The full details of the new FCA's Enforcement Powers can be found at http://www.fca.org.uk/static/documents/enforcement-information-guide.pdf

Chapter 14: Compliance Risk Assessment

Domestically, the Financial Reporting Council has now published a new (Sept 2012) edition of the "UK Corporate Governance Code" and it also updated and published "The UK Stewardship Code", both originally published in 2010. The Financial Services Authority (FSA) Chief Executive Hector Sants's made a speech on 17 June 2010 to the Chartered Institute of Securities and Investments (CISI) conference drew attention to the importance of a firm's culture in developing good regulatory outcomes and the role that governance plays in this.

Since December 2010 all UK-authorised Asset Managers are required under the FSA's Conduct of Business Rules to produce a statement of commitment to the Stewardship Code or explain why it is not appropriate to their business model.

Sir David Walker's Review made several recommendations including the role of the Chief Risk Officer and the establishment of Risk Committees and the temptation of many firms will be to say "we are too small to consider risk officers or committees", or using the regulator's term of appropriate and proportionate would claim that they are not of significant size, turnover or risk rating to warrant such attention. In some cases this may be true but in many it could be a false assumption. There could be a number of items that get overlooked because you have been running the business for years and are "on top of everything." Unfortunately a number of firms have found that they are often lacking in Systems & Controls (SYSC) requirements, even Article 3 Exempt firms, which quickly become apparent after a themed visit from the regulator and a Section 166 Report "Requirements Notice" dropping into their inbox. This can be avoided and our eBook, "**A General Guide to S166 Reports**", is available from Compliance Consultant website (www.complianceconsultant.org) and YouTube.com, may help avert such actions.

Risk assessment can be difficult to anyone who is too close to the business. However, that said, it is not impossible and often a good 75% can be done effectively in this way. It is often best to get a third party, such as your Compliance Consultant to check over the work done, just as you would expect a quality assurance check on people who check files.

If you plan your activity and spend time using each step properly and thoroughly then you will form the basis of a Compliance Risk Register (CRR), supporting document to your Management Information (MI) and provide a dashboard for presenting/reporting to the other senior managers within the firm. This also provides a handy tool (historic and contemporary) for any regulatory visits and keeps you focussed on the higher risk elements and any that are nearing your Compliance Risk Appetite (CRA). This not only makes good business sense but also helps to show you have considered the elements to demonstrate that you are Treating Customers Fairly (TCF), specifically Outcomes 1 & 2. A free **"Guide for TCF self-appraisal"** is available on request from our website (www.complianceconsultant.org).

PHASE 1 – Data Collection

Step One: Products and Services, employment and production environment

Make a list of all products and services that are offered. These could include any Mortgage, General Insurance as well as Life and Pensions or Investment products, Will writing referrals, Tax Planning, business or personal loans, Debt Counselling or any areas that your firm is involved in.

Step Two: Systems and Controls

If necessary, meet with Departmental Management or the Office Manager (depending on size) to identify what types of company or department policies, procedures, systems, and automation are in place? List these carefully as they form your controls.

- Interview Department Management to identify controls
    - Policies and procedures to maintain compliance
    - Degree to which processes are centralised or decentralised
    - Degree to which processes are automated or manual
    - Location where these products/services are sold
    - Location where the customers of these products/services are located
    - Degree of staff turnover
    - Training to maintain compliance
    - Are there plans for new products/services?
    - Have there been any changes in the product/service/controls in the past year?
        - If so describe
    - What about your Disaster Recovery/Business Continuity plans?
    - How is your IT managed?
- Summarise your controls
- Meet again to ensure that you have a complete and accurate summary of controls (and not just your interpretation)

Step Three: Applicable Regulations

With the list of products and services, produce a table where you can record any primary regulations that apply to the products and services offered? This is known as mapping your regulatory territory (see Chapter 8) and is not restricted to just FCA rules. There are Advertising Standards Authority rules to consider as well as new and existing legislation concerning the business right down to employment and other obligations to consider.

- Identify the primary regulations that apply to the list you have formed in Step One.

PHASE 2 – Inherent Risk Analysis

Whatever you do today there is risk. There is a risk of companies defaulting, there are risks concerned with service level agreements not being honoured, and there are risks that clients may not fully understand the range of products you advise on and it is important to redouble your controls in these areas, for obvious reasons.

Step One: Regulatory Risk

The regulator has "hot buttons" and these may be Unregistered Collective Investment Schemes (UCIS), the new Non-readily Realisable Securities (NRRS) or it may be Structured Products and the guarantees offered. You need to be aware of the regulator's expectations for compliance in the areas you operate in? What issues are at the top of their current list? What is the complexity of the regulatory requirements or is there a lack of specific regulatory guidance.

Risk rating these areas will help you form a potential identifier for where you may need to concentrate your efforts in risk mitigation. The Financial Ombudsman Service (FOS) Report is a good indicator of things that people complain about. Check it out and relate it to your business, products or services.

Although this is provided as guidance you could define further levels and it is often useful to attach a monetary or number of customers value to them (as appropriate) so that you can start to form a risk appetite.

Risk elements to consider are;
- Low –
    - None or minor penalties or consequences;

- o Not a current regulatory priority;
- o Noncomplex requirement
- o Not an area that we generally have issues with
- Medium –
    - o Potential for moderate penalties and/or consequences;
    - o Currently a moderate focus or priority for regulators
    - o Moderately complex with incomplete regulatory guidance
    - o Periodic errors noted by examiners and testers
- High –
    - o Potential for significant penalties and/or consequences
    - o Currently a high priority of regulators
    - o Highly complex requirement with incomplete regulatory guidance
    - o One of the leading areas where errors are noted

Step Two: Reputation Risk

What is the level of public and customer concern/publicity over noncompliance?
- Low – No or low concern likely;
- Medium – Moderate concern possible;
- High – Significant concern or loss of customer confidence likely

Step Three: Inherent Risk

Using the regulatory risk and reputation risk identified in steps 1 and 2, what is the inherent risk in each product and service?

Inherent risk is defined as the risk before any controls are exercised or effected? Rank the risk by Regulatory Risk and Reputation Risk.

High Regulatory Risk	Medium	High	High
Medium Regulatory Risk	Low	Medium	High
Low Regulatory Risk	Low	Low	Medium
INHERENT RISK	Low Reputation Risk	Medium Reputation Risk	High Regulatory Risk

PHASE 3 Residual Risk Analysis

Step One: Operational Risk

Although this can often be subjective, we have found it best carried out with at least two people, preferably as a workshop. These are only guidelines and can be amended by you as required.

Simply evaluate the risk associated with: the presence or absence of internal controls, processes, and procedures to maintain compliance; the degree of centralisation or decentralisation; level of automation to eliminate human error; staff turnover that could contribute to errors; and existence of adequate training, annual testing or other competence measures.

- Low –
    - Presence of good internal controls, processes, and procedures to maintain compliance
    - Centralised
    - Partially or fully automated
    - Low staff turnover
    - Adequate training has been provided

- o Account opened Face-to-Face on site (no distance sales)
- ➢ Customer is local, (lives/works)
- Medium –
  - o Some weaknesses or soft areas in internal controls, processes, or procedures
  - o Partially decentralised
  - o Some automation
  - o Moderate staff turnover
  - o Minimal training provided infrequently
  - o Account opened Face-to-Face off site (no distance sales)
- ➢ Customer located relatively local (within 100 miles) and is maintained adequately
- High –
  - o Weak or no internal controls, processes or procedures
  - o Decentralized
  - o Not automated
  - o High staff turnover
  - o No training provided
  - o Account not opened Face-to-Face
- ➢ Customer located over 100 miles away and much business is done by phone/fax/email.

Step Two: Probability of Error Risk

Evaluate the risk that error will occur due to prior history of error and changes in regulatory requirements, products, and/or services.

Test/Audit/Exam Results
- Low – No errors in last review;
- Moderate – Minor errors in last review;
- High – Significant errors in last review

Change in regulatory requirements
- Low – No changes since last monitored;
- Moderate – Minor changes since last monitored;
- High – Significant changes since last monitored

Change in product / service
- Low – No changes since last monitored;
- Moderate – Minor changes since last monitored;
- High – Significant changes since last monitored

Step Three: Residual Risk

Using the information gathered in steps 1 and 2, what is the residual risk in each product and service? That is, what is the risk after controls? Rank the risk by Operational Risk and Probability of Error Risk, which is the likelihood that an error will occur.

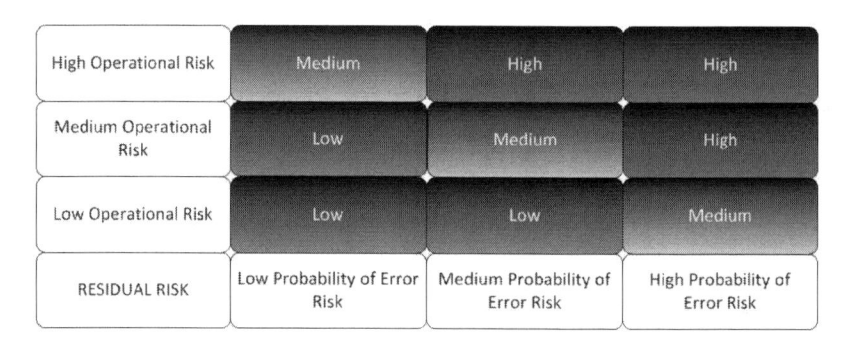

High Operational Risk	Medium	High	High
Medium Operational Risk	Low	Medium	High
Low Operational Risk	Low	Low	Medium
RESIDUAL RISK	Low Probability of Error Risk	Medium Probability of Error Risk	High Probability of Error Risk

Phase 4 Overall Risk Analysis and Follow-up

Step One: Overall Risk

At this point, the risks can be charted on a sliding scale by product or service. For example:

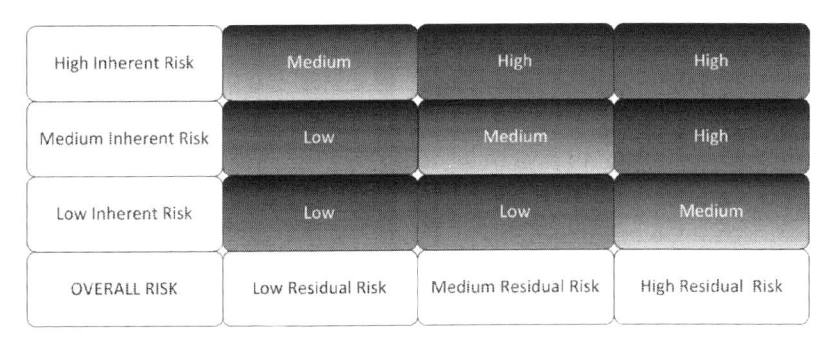

High Inherent Risk	Medium	High	High
Medium Inherent Risk	Low	Medium	High
Low Inherent Risk	Low	Low	Medium
OVERALL RISK	Low Residual Risk	Medium Residual Risk	High Residual Risk

Where the words Low, Moderate and High Appear, will be the product or service name(s). At this point, the chart can be colour coded so that cells that show Low Risk are Yellow; cells showing Moderate are Orange and cells showing High are Red. This provides information "at a glance" for management, the business lines and regulators.

Step Two: Management Tolerance of Compliance Risk

What is management's tolerance (risk appetite) of compliance risk? Are there instances where overall risk can be high, despite controls, and still be acceptable to management? If so, document why. If management's appetite for risk is low, the adequacy of controls must be rigorously monitored to ensure that residual risk is low. Note that the risk may be different by product or service. Take that into consideration along with management's overall view of compliance risk.

Step Three: Direction of Risk

Consider the direction of risk and probable change in risk over the next twelve months. Categorise this for each product and service using the definitions listed below.

Increasing	Management should take additional action through more controls or increased reviews
Stable	No additional action is required
Decreasing	Management may want to consider decreasing controls and improving efficiencies

This provides an overview of risk management at a practical level for Compliance Managers. For greater Risk Management Practice with examples and step by step instructions we recommend you read "*ARMS – Analysis and Risk Management System*" or if you are an IFA, "*IFARM – IFA Risk Management*", both available at Amazon for Kindle or at www.leewerrell.co.uk/blog .

NRRS details and the new "Restricted Investor" category explanations can be found in PS14/4 on the FCA Website http://www.fca.org.uk/static/documents/policy-statements/ps14-04.pdf

Chapter 15: Regulatory Visit Preparation

Whilst there could be any regulator that decides to pay a visit to monitor the activities of your firm, we will primarily deal with the new methodology and if the sections or items do not apply to the notified visit you are to receive, then ignore them or scale them down accordingly.

The Advanced Risk Responsive Operating frameWork (ARROW) review was developed by the FSA and provided the framework for a full-on regulatory visit. Understanding the original process may help you appreciate the new regime as there are two major benefits. Firstly, Firms historically have so obviously been wildly underprepared for regulatory visits that this should help you realise the need to prepare and secondly that there is an increased momentum and lower tolerance accepted by the FCA.

Whilst maintaining the "Principle Based Regulation" strategy, there has been a demonstrable rise in FCA monitoring and they have adopted a graduated interventionist approach representing a 'tougher and more intrusive regulation'. The FCA has also abandoned the ARROW model and has opted for thematic reviews and "Deep Dives" into areas within specific firms and their operations. Firms can expect a much more probing and aggressive approach by the regulator with more weight on conduct than prudential management.

Building on the lessons learned from the Northern Rock review, Hector Sants, the FSA's CEO at the time, outlined the regulator's intentions to implement a more intrusive and intensive style of supervision, explaining that "The FSA has moved firmly into the realm of making judgments on judgements. Wrongdoers should be afraid of the FSA".

It *should not* be considered automatic that a poor outcome from a regulatory review or even a thematic visit will automatically lead to a S166 Report as there are a number of options available to the FCA. Enforcement activities could include;

- imposition of intensive remedial action (via the Risk Mitigation Programme);
- impact on the Firm's relationship with the FCA (i.e. more intensive monitoring);
- section 165 Requiring information to be provided;
- section 167 Appointment to carry out general investigations
- section 168 Appointment to carry out particular investigations
- Including actions against individuals (senior management/directors).
- other enforcement actions with extreme cases a Firm being placed on the FCA Firm Watch List.

Due to the changes in the Financial Services and Markets Act 2000 (FSMA), the Financial Conduct Authority (FCA) have an extensive range of disciplinary, criminal and civil powers to take action against regulated and non-regulated firms and individuals who are failing or have failed to meet the standards they require.

Examples of their powers include being able to:

- withdraw a firm's authorisation;
- prohibit an individual from operating in financial services;
- prevent an individual from undertaking specific regulated activities;
- suspend a firm for up to 12 months from undertaking specific regulated activities;
- suspend an individual for up to two years from undertaking specific controlled functions;
- censure firms and individuals through public statements;
- impose financial penalties;

- seek injunctions;
- apply to court to freeze assets;
- seek restitution orders; and
- prosecute firms and individuals who undertake regulated activities without authorisation

The FCA have said that they will work very closely with other law enforcement agencies.

Total Cost of S166 Reports

In June 2010, the regulator obtained new powers, Financial Services Act 2010. Although use of these are unlikely to directly arise from a visit, there could well be areas that the FCA may want to investigate further. The new powers are;

- new suspension powers for both firms (section 206A) and approved persons (section 66)
- new power to impose penalties on persons that perform controlled functions without approval, under section 63A of FSMA
- restriction on imposing a financial penalty and withdrawing a person's authorisation in section 206(2) of FSMA has been removed
- extension for taking action against an approved person for misconduct in section 66(4) from two to three years
- new power to impose financial penalties on persons who breach short selling rules under section 131G of FSMA

Is the common myth that there will be a dramatic increase in use of S166 true?

FCA and PRA have published on their website the latest number of Skilled Persons Reviews ("SPR") or Section 166 ("S166") from 1 April 2013 to 30 September 2013, there were 47 S166 issued by both FCA and PRA in total. Although they have the power to appoint SPR directly, only 5 were contracted directly up until 30 September 2013.

In 2010, 14 Life Companies were issued with S166 Reports, 9 Banks, 23 IFAs and 7 Hedge Fund or Asset Managers as well as interdealer brokers and mortgage companies. The total cost was £24.8 million and the most expensive review was £4.4 million, resulting in a median cost for all firms of £128,000.

In 2008 there were just 30 S166 Reports, in 2009 this rose to 56 and this latest increase sets the trend onto an exponential curve.

Note: Compliance Consultants can often provide a better and more cost effective service than larger organisations as they have skilled staff to hand, have more experience per consultant and can assess processes and procedures, as well as governance and risk elements.

Remember: If you have any concerns regarding any compliance issues, please contact an independent consultant who is a member of the Association of Professional Compliance Consultants (APCC), recognised as a trade body by the FCA.

Hot topics for the FCA can be gleaned from the Annual FCA Risk Outlook, published around the end of the first quarter each year for the year ahead.

The Starting Point

A more 'direct and intrusive approach' to supervision has been the warning sent out from the FCA over the last twelve months. Firms and individuals are rightly concerned that as a result of reviews increasing in their intensity the FCA themselves are much better prepared and more skilled in a wider range of business models and categories now, resulting in a much more robust challenge with increased emphasis on risk rating and benchmarking.

The FCA itself is showing that it is preparing more thoroughly for acting fast where enforcement action may be required. The FCA has included technical specialists as members of their visit team and appears to be viewing firms as part of an overall sector and systemic themed approach, rather than the previously more individualised stance. This has been further demonstrated by half of firms experiencing an increase in the number of pre-visit documents requested, and the documentation sent was seen to have been considered thoroughly by the FCA.

A themed visit is not designed to catch you out or to tell you how to run your business specifically, and it is possible for firms to avoid sustaining any 'injury' or unwelcome outcome from an FCA review. Firms and individuals can be proactive and take action to prepare not only for the review process but to embed a culture within the firm that encompasses best practice, compliant behaviours and risk awareness.

The regulatory themed review involves anything from an online questionnaire, a telephone or face to face interview or an on-site inspection visit focusing on a firm's systems and controls, entire risk management and governance. The Risk assessment considers the impact and probability of failure. The impact assessment is determined by the size of the firm and its sector and the probability assessment determines the approach to the type of supervision a firm can expect going forward.

Early Planning for any assessment

Like the famous Boy Scouts Motto, the key to any regulatory visit, and particularly a regulatory review; even if remotely conducted, you should "Be prepared" and be prepared as early as you can, being proactive as soon as you can. Awaiting the receipt of the initial notification can often be too late.

It's always best to engage your Compliance Consultant as early on as possible if you are not used to this type of intervention as they know what to expect and the best ways to position the firm to the regulator.

Typically Firms will receive ample notice of a routine regulatory visit, but this can be severely cut short if the visit is part of an investigation. If the latter is the case, although not in all cases, the chances are you have probably been involved in the lead up to the investigation anyhow.

- The notice should clearly state or, you should try to clarify;
- The reason for the visit;
- The matters to be reviewed (themed visit or Deep Dive?);
- The documents and records to be reviewed (documentation request and for on-site visit);
- The category and number of people to be interviewed;
- The number and function of the regulators staff and their roles.

There are times when the timing of the visit is just not practical due to key staff absence due to holidays or sabbaticals, maternity leave etc., inspection by another regulatory body or locally holiday "shutdowns" (less likely these days, but still a consideration) mean that administrative staff may well be thin on the ground.

The first step is to appoint a project sponsor, and this will usually be the person responsible for Compliance. It is critical that your senior management buy in to this process not only making it a high priority but also aligning and committing resources.

Secondly, appoint a cross function Project team (or maybe just one person) who is likely to be an office manager or someone who knows the administration system, the advisers, governance procedures and even elements of the risk practices. Your Firm should be able to demonstrate good corporate governance and that their risk management processes and practices are embedded throughout the organisation. The aim is for Firms to demonstrate that the key risks faced by the Firm as a whole and by each part of the Firm are identified, understood and recorded and that mitigating controls are in place. Although senior management responsibility has been a long-held tenet of the FCA, there is an increasing focus by FCA to hold individuals to account. We provide a separate Compliance Risk Assessment Guide free on request.

Thirdly, your entire staff will need to know what an FCA Review is, what it means to the firm and how they are to respond. People are normally protective of their family and their working environment and may well be tempted to put up a false front with anything they think is not important: this needs to be explained to them in detail, perhaps over a series of briefings, more frequently as the visit date approaches. Point to note here is that if you have any outsourced functions at all, the proper documentation and requirements are in place as per FCA Handbook Senior Management Arrangements, Systems and Controls (SYSC) Chapter 8.

Business process documentation should be complete and up-to-date. An important part of the review preparation, to be undertaken several months in advance, is to identify where there may be deficiencies and 'getting the house in order' with respect to business controls, audit and record keeping. Prior to receiving the interview or information request it is useful to think about the information that may be requested.

Typically this will include Board and Committee Minutes for the previous 12 months; Organisation Chart; Management Information Packs for at least 6 or even 12 months; Business Plans including strategy and financial plans for at least this year but typically next 2-3; Business Continuity Plans, not just where you store the computer records; Compliance Monitoring Programmes and internal audit reports up to perhaps the last three years, Complaints records, Risk Register, ICAP/ICAS, RMARs and other regulatory submissions. However the information requests can also include details of Board attendance, details on outsourcing agreements and, increasingly, information on product lifecycle.

Firms should have conducted an assessment of the strengths and weaknesses of their own risk capabilities and show how these have been addressed prior to the review. There should be no surprises.

Don't be in a rush to send the documentation off as soon as part of it is obtained. Before you respond you should ensure that the documentation is carefully prepared, clear and complete, labelled clearly and even with separators to make sure nothing is mixed up with other documents. Information should be accurate, current and appropriately signed off according to your matrix of authority or other documented internal process. This part of the process is critical to creating the best impression. You should use a third party (external Compliance Consultancy) to critically review the information – are there gaps/weaknesses, what further questions does it raise, does it demonstrate sound governance and effective risk management practices or does it appear like a mish-mash of things thrown together? All of these elements have to be robust, cohesive and congruent with your firms practice. Any attempt at manufacturing, amending or otherwise "tidying" up will be spotted a mile off. Is there an appropriate quantity and quality of management information and evidence of effective decision making and monitoring? Are the right judgements being made? Are the decisions fully documented and annotated accordingly? Have policies been reviewed recently, amended and is there evidence of their approval? Is version control used for all documentation, including customer facing documents?

Points to note, which may cause anxiety are; any areas where the firm is unclear as to exactly what the FCA requires should be followed up as soon as possible. A copy (or ensure easy reproduction) should be maintained of all submissions to the FCA, together with all other recent submissions, e.g., RMAR and transaction reporting data. All your senior managers should be made aware of the information requested by and submitted to the FCA. You should also be aware that any documentation requested is likely to form the basis of at least some interview questions. Nearer to the time of the visit the interviewees themselves should understand and be familiar with the information which has been provided. Some coaching in formal interviews may also be needed for individuals and it may be worth considering hiring an HR professional or trainer to conduct sessions at your offices. All interviewees should be aware of relevant evidence and examples to demonstrate how governance and risk management works in the organisation and to show how significant decisions have been made, relevant to their role.

The FCA focus will be obviously be specific to the Firm, the sector and generic "hot topics". A part of the pre-visit planning will be to identify what areas the FCA will focus on and anticipate the questions they may ask. Don't forget the FCA are practiced at using questions and use a three level approach generally.

To forearm yourself, you may consider familiarizing yourself with not only the FCA Latest Publications, but with the various helpful PDFs and guides. Other general areas of interest may be obtained from FCA sector briefings, discussion and consultation papers, the current Financial Risk Outlook, FCA business plan; and Dear CEO letters. In addition, Industry groups, colleagues/contacts in other firms and professional advisors will have a view as to what are the current hot topics. An important point to remember is that a peer group comparison will be included in the letter, so understanding what types of Firm the FCA will consider as your peers and how you measure up against them will assist in planning for any other visit. Be warned: The FCA allocated Peer group may not include who you think - peer groups can be allocated by business mix, location or the FCA regulatory remit.

A common misconception appears to be that the FCA are limited to the information and material provided by the firm at the time of the documentation request. In fact, their sources of information are varied and can include any previous Risk Mitigation Plans (and progress made on implementation of these), ICAAP/ICAS reviews and any Internal Capital Guidance letters, the FCA relationship manager (if any), whistle-blower claims, internet searches, social media (Facebook, Twitter, Digg etc.) as well as senior management who have previously been involved in reviews or have otherwise interacted with the FCA, will provide some insight into the specific area of concern for the Firm in the upcoming review. There is always the intelligence provided by the general public and industry professionals who may come across something and report it to the regulator.

Preparing for the Review

Avoiding surprises

If, during the pre-visit planning, there are weaknesses identified or even breaches or any other red flags, how will these be dealt with? Senior managers should be aware of any and all action points either raised previously by the FCA or identified by the firm as part of its ongoing monitoring, and the work done to rectify the issues. Correct ownership must be taken and steps taken to demonstrate the issue is under active management and evidence of ongoing resolution should be to hand. It is important to show that this is being treated as business as usual, not as a one off for the visit. A strong risk culture with Risk and Compliance fully engaged throughout the business.

Increasingly important is the role that Management Information (MI) has to play in the running of regulated firms today. You need to be able to ensure that senior managers can justify the content, inherent assumptions and frequency of MI in order to be able to demonstrate that it is effective and fit for purpose. In addition, firms should be able to show how MI is generated and then used to drive decisions and actions.

There should be a clear definition of key elements of how the business is run and managed.
- the strategic priorities for the business;
- the main risks to the firm and how they are identified;

- how risk appetite is determined;
- the challenge processes that are built into the risk framework;
- how the effectiveness of the corporate governance framework is assessed;
- how the firm knows that it is treating customers fairly;
- how the culture of the firm would be described;
- operation and effectiveness of the risk, compliance and audit functions providing lines of defence; and
- what could make the firm fail and what are the indicators and mitigating factors.

With all the preparation in the world, the outcome is crucially dependent on ensuring that interviewees provide clear, accurate information about the areas on which they have knowledge. The interviewees should feel comfortable in commenting that they do not work in an area or have no working knowledge if they really don't. The areas they have knowledge or competency in they should be easily able to comment and effectively demonstrate the controls within the firm.

Confirm with the FCA Team coordinator if they wish or will permit a member of compliance to also attend the interviews, and if so, ensure that you have a suitably senior and knowledgeable member of the department available for the more senior, if not all of the interviews.

Anyone whom may be selected for interview should:
- Give clear, brief answers
- Stick to the remit of their role and not try to guess or answer wider questions if unsure.

- They should avoid letting personal opinions or ego get in the way of factual answers.

- Be able to evidence that major decisions, e.g., around strategy and risk appetite, are being discussed at board meetings and effectively challenged rather than simply rubber-stamped.

- If they are not senior management, they should be able to explain how decisions are disseminated through the firm.

- Don't use unfamiliar terminology: if they don't know, ask what is meant.

Executives need to be able to explain and demonstrate how the firm's governance process works and more specifically articulate the level of risk appetite and how this affects business decisions.

Executives should also show awareness and be able to explain clearly what elements or events could bring the business down and what is being done to offset those risks.

Compliance Consultant (info@complianceconsultant.org) provides an executive training program and this can be provided as a crash course if needed.

This is not a memory test, notebooks or other documents can be taken in with you.

All interviewees would do well to use the meeting with the FCA as an opportunity to demonstrate how they have correctly and accurately discharged the obligations of their role. While this is obviously critical for approved persons it sets a strong example at all levels of the firm.

It would be worth noting that if an individual interviewee is unavailable on the required day, the FCA may conduct the interview later at its Canary Wharf offices, which can be more stressful.

The Visit - What is expected

Your project team, and indeed all staff, by the dawning of the first day of the visit, should be able to articulate the desired outcome of the review visit and the firm's key messages to the FCA.

Organisation and smooth running, provision of extra information and timeliness of persons appearing for interview is essential during the visit to ensure that the review can be undertaken as quickly and smoothly as possible. This is so often overlooked by many firms and can be easily facilitated.

A good idea is to;
- Consider assigning an administrative manager for the visit to keep executives on time for interviews, arrange for the provision of files, refreshments, photocopying, access to systems and to act as general liaison point between the firm and the FCA visit team. An office manager or team leader would be best suited: who know not only the system but who to contact when it doesn't work.
- Ensure availability of significant people for interview.
- Book interview rooms and a secure room for the FCA to work in.

As previously explained it is important that you maintain records of information that you have provided to the regulator and as part of this it is advisable to keep records of meetings and interviews that take place as part of the visit. The FCA will normally allow note-takers to attend the meetings but you should confirm that this is permitted and ask about the acceptability of using recording equipment, if it is considered applicable.

On a daily basis you should seek to have a daily debrief with the FCA and circulate the results to senior managers. It may also be possible to provide updates in the gaps between the FCA interviews.

As we have seen over the last few months, the FCA has been placing much more emphasis on the role of senior management in its reviews. The outcomes-focussed regulatory approach represents less reliance on systems and controls as the days when the FCA relied on management to make the right judgement have long gone. Today the FCA will question the judgement and rationale of decisions of senior managers and take action if their actions have led to unacceptable risks.

Executives and Non-Executive Directors are expected to not only be able to articulate clearly how governance structures work across the organisation but how these structures are appropriate and effective in the Firm's model and how they personally provide an active challenge to management, preferably with examples. For smaller companies the emphasis is on risk appraisal, risk mitigation and controls.

As you may have gathered, advisers are not the prime candidates for interviews these days and there appears to be not only an increased number but also a much wider range of interviewees such as the role and effectiveness of Non-Executive Directors and a move to include junior level personnel in any interviews. Administration staff may also be questioned about a variety of issues and operational challenges they encounter on a day to day basis.

Increasingly the scope of interviews is also becoming much widely reported.

The FCA wants to see a firm which is capable of realistically assessing risks facing it from all quarters, the effective and timely reporting on those risks and their proposed or actual mitigation. The FCA is very likely to be interested in how you, as a company, define risk appetite and places risks in the context of that risk appetite. The FCA will want to see a firm which is not afraid to identify and escalate deficiencies or problems, employ speedy and expert advice, willing to discuss solutions and monitor delivery of those solutions and, in particular, is willing and able to learn from mistakes.

Key Points for Consideration

It cannot be reiterated enough or too often that for you to obtain the best result from any regulatory review or any themed visit, briefings and mock interviews with individual coaching and feedback are among the best tools that can be used to assist the individuals to successfully engage with the FCA.

Typically this process would be led by Compliance and may involve the use of outside compliance and risk solution consultants (as a fresh set of eyes and to provide an objective viewpoint and additional experiential information). Individuals should be able to address risks and issues not only in their area of direct responsibility but also in their role as a manager of a business area or function and as a member of the leadership team, boards and committees. They should be able to reconcile these roles within a Firm-wide view of the Risk Management Process providing evidence and examples where possible.

Preparation should not ignore simple interview techniques - body language and attitude can impact how the interview proceeds. For some individuals the interview process can be intimidating - simple coaching and prior preparation can go a long way to relieve anxiety.

Do agree on the presence of note-takers in advance. These individuals should be able to quickly identify emerging key points/possible areas of concern and their role should be to identify issues as the review process progresses, brief management and prepare those yet to be interviewed. Note takers should have a close of day de-brief with the project team. At the conclusion of the visit a Firm should ask for a close out meeting assess initial reactions, clear up any factual inaccuracies and determine whether any further documentation or interviews are needed.

Whilst the inspection process may not be a welcome one, full cooperation with the FCA team is expected. Firms are encouraged to engage with the FCA in a proactive and open-minded matter (Principle 11). The inspection team should be provided with interview rooms, and a space to work with access to telephone, refreshments, and access to copying facilities as well as any systems to view documents "online".

The FCA will have a team of two or often more people. FCA Specialists are often called in to drill down (Deep Dive) in a particular area and scrutinise a Firm's business activities and risk management practices. The FCA may have two teams on site at any one time, with one conducting interviews while the other makes notes of completed interviews and prepares for the next. In some cases enforcement staff have been included and inspection teams have sat in on board meetings and risk committee meetings.

Next Steps

Following the review visit, a Firm should agree with the FCA the timing of the FCA follow up and clarify its understanding of the messages given; agreeing on what the on-going communication with the FCA should be up to the receipt of the draft report letter.

A draft Risk Mitigation Programme (RMP) will normally be drawn up by the FCA team and you should be sure to ask for a copy to ensure that any factual inaccuracies within the RMP can be followed up.

You may wish to consider appointing a RMP resolution manager to oversee the coordination of the activities, responsibilities and reporting to the FCA, or if you are a SME then the Compliance Officer will normally fulfil this function. There should follow a specific full board discussion on the issues raised and the resources required for remediation. It may be a good idea to invite a compliance consultancy to attend the discussion to take notes and offer advice on any rectification actions needed. A lot of the work will be easily undertaken internally, but it is important to deal with the issues as a whole rather than separate non-cohesive elements.

A vitally important part of the RMP process is to keep and maintain a full documentary record of all actions taken, together with the responsible, agreed timescales for correcting issues and supporting evidence to show that new and fully functioning controls have been put in place, or existing controls have been improved, to prevent any issue identified from recurring.

If you are a member of a group, or a part of a foreign owned company, you should give due consideration to external notification of head offices, parent companies and overseas regulators, where applicable, the results of the visit and a follow up remedial action plan if necessary.

Before the dust settles, but after everyone has had a chance to exhale and reflect on their experience, hold a workshop (on or offsite) and review the visit and of what went well and any lessons to be learned.

Once received, the draft letter should be reviewed for factual accuracy, and evidence provided where this is not the case – this is the only part of the letter a Firm is allowed to comment on and can influence after the interview have completed. Firms must ensure that the priorities and issues are clear to them in the Risk Mitigation Programme. This should be submitted to the board with a clear plan of action, including resources required, timescales for addressing issues, measures to prevent any issues reoccurring, and how and what controls will be implemented. All actions will need to be fully documented with regular progress reports put in place.

How Do We Know If We Are Looking at Enforcement Action?

From your daily meetings and your close out meeting you will have a strong feeling of where the RMP is going or the general flavour. Obviously some areas will require further investigation which will be conducted normally off-site. All evidence (or lack of it) is cited in the report.

The key elements that the FCA use to determine enforcement referral are;
- Has there been actual or potential consumer loss/detriment?
- Is there evidence of financial crime or risk of financial crime?
- Are there actions or potential breaches that could undermine public confidence in the orderliness of financial markets?
- Are there issues that indicate a widespread problem or weakness at the firm/issuer?
- Is there evidence that the firm/issuer/individual has profited from the action or potential breaches?
- Has the firm/issuer/individual failed to bring the actions or potential breaches to the attention of the FCA?
- Is the issue to be referred relevant to an FCA strategic priority?
- If the issue does not fall within an FCA strategic priority, does the conduct in question make the conduct particularly egregious and presenting a serious risk to one of the FCA's objectives?
- What was the reaction of the firm/issuer/individual to the breach?
- Overall, is the use of the enforcement tool likely to further the FCA's aims and Objectives?
- Does the suspected misconduct involve an overseas jurisdiction? If so, would enforcement action materially further investor protection or market confidence in that jurisdiction?

What can they do about it?
- Financial penalties and public censures

- Private warnings
- Variation and cancellation of Part IV permission
- Prohibition orders and withdrawal of approval
- Suspensions
- Injunctive action
- Restitution and redress
- Criminal prosecution
- Insolvency
- Collective Investment Schemes
- Disqualification of auditors and actuaries
- Disapplication orders against members of the professions
- Cancellation of Sponsor approval
- Non-FSMA powers

In most cases where a lack of controls are found, or there are minor breaches and bad practices a period of enhanced supervision is recommended with regular reporting to the FCA and a significant increase on management time and focus.

The next stage could easily be a specific S166 Report on a designated area of suspect operation. Don't forget that under Part XI of the FSMA, a Section 166 Skilled Person's Reports can be used, in the FCA's examples in SUP 5 Annex 1 for a single or any mix of;

- Diagnostic
- Diagnostic / monitoring
- Monitoring
- Preventative
- Remedial

These are not restricted to the firm today either. The Report can cover;
- all firms (all authorised persons under section 31 FSMA)
- any other member of the firm's group
- a partnership of which the firm is a member
- a person who has at any relevant time been a person falling within the above (where such person was carrying on a business)

In this overview we have offered a number of common sense tips on how to improve the chances of both the Firm as a whole and individuals in obtaining their objectives for a successful outcome from a regulatory review visit, whether as part of a wider thematic review or a Deep Dive. Early preparation is important to ensure that you are totally ready for the visit, with sound Governance and Risk Management arrangements in place. Appointing a project team with clear responsibilities within the context of a clearly articulated and understood objective for success as well as ongoing dialogue between that team and the FCA are also important if your organisation allows that level of resource. Finally, proper preparation (briefings. mock interviews, feedback) are also tried and tested ways of maximising the likelihood of success. Although we cannot cater for all models and sizes of business, we hope this has provided you with a more thorough insight into what is involved.

In summary; whenever you are dealing with any compliance event, breach or issue, or if you are subject to regulatory scrutiny, consider the following areas.
- Take control of the problem in so far as possible
- Analyse the issue – but do so with the benefit of legal advice
- Privilege and protected items S413 – the role of compliance

- Do not create hostages to fortune – the dangers of email and text messages
- Take action to ensure problem cannot recur
- Review systems and controls
- Consider remediation/compensation of customer losses
- Consider disciplinary action against employees – but consider consequences carefully. Dismissal may deprive you of access to important information
- Consider the need for employees to have separate advice and fund that advice
- Show FCA you are being pro-active in dealing with the issue
- Try to stay one step ahead of the FCA by anticipating their requirements
- Other investigations/litigation and their outcomes.

Chapter 16: Compliance Activities

This brief chapter will describe some of the routine activities most commonly undertaken by the Compliance Manager. Please remember that this guidance provides a summation only and you should tailor the various procedures and controls within your own firm to the requirements of your business activities, permissions and customer offerings.

Maintenance of your compliance manual

The maintenance of your compliance manual is one of the main tools that you will be using throughout each year and although there is no regulatory requirement in the UK for firms to have a compliance manual there is, a regulatory expectation that such a document exists. The main benefit of this document is that it can contain the relevant points of your compliance regime as well as summarise or explain company policies, status, company vision and mission statements as well as responsibilities of members of staff.

The manual acts as an insurance policy for you as long as you ensure that all new joiners have some kind of method to confirm they have read and understood impact on their position and it is also recommended to instigate an annual attestation or other form of proof should there be any major changes to the manual.

The manual should be written as a fairly high level and if greater detail is required references to the company policies should be made with a précis of the policy contained in the manual providing a workable explanation. Nobody including you is going to read a war and peace type manual however there are a number of considerations of areas that can be input.

Your manual should ideally contain at least the sections listed (alphabetically):

- Advertising for New Business
- Anti-Money Laundering

- Breaches, Discipline & Enforcement
- Bribery, Facilitation and Unethical Payments
- Business Continuity
- Client classification
- Company introduction and areas of business
- Company's compliance structure
- Complaints handling & procedure
- Complaints Sample Logs (General, EONWD, RFCs)
- Conduct Risk
- Conflicts of Interest
- Controlled Functions and Governance
- Customer Assets
- Data Protection
- Data Protection & Employees Rights
- Dealing with Customers
- FCA Principles for Business
- Financial Promotions
- High Level Regulatory Requirements
- Inducements/Gifts and Entertaining
- Introduction and responsibilities of staff
- Market Abuse & Insider Dealing
- Notifications to the FCA
- Outsourcing
- Principles & Code of Practice for Approved Persons

- Record Keeping
- Regulatory environment and Scope of permissions overview
- Remuneration
- Risk assessment
- Senior Management Systems and Controls
- Senior Staff/Management listing
- Specific Permissions for company
- Table of Contents
- Terms of Business
- Training & Competence
- Treating Customers Fairly (TCF) - Overview
- Treating Customers Fairly (TCF) - Application
- Version Control log
- Whistle-blowing

If you have an intranet this would ideally be located there either as a separate section or as a downloadable PDF. Ensure that full version control is adhered to.

Maintenance of compliance policies and procedures

Obviously the points here to consider are that all the policies have been reviewed on a regular basis and include best practice and any references for external legislation or guidance such as the Joint Money Laundering Steering Group (JMLSG) and ensure that the correct level of detail is included especially in policies such as whistleblowing, fraud and data security.

Increasingly governance is falling to the compliance officer to monitor and maintain and you should make yourself familiar with all policies, owners of policies, terms of reference (TORs) and any risk management program so that you can consider any impact on these if any events unfold.

If there is an area where you consider a policy or a written procedure would be beneficial then write the appropriate document and submitted to the board for approval. If your firm is part of a group you may need to consider tying this in the group policies and procedures. Be aware that money laundering and conflicts of interest policies should be written on a firm specific basis as covering a group that may have diverse operations would require a policy to be too high level.

Please remember if you instigate a new policy then training for the affected staff will also have to be scheduled and the policy will need to be built into the annual compliance monitoring plan.

Annual compliance monitoring plan

The objective of the annual compliance monitoring plan is to provide a review of all matters that fall under the compliance focus on a scheduled plan throughout a 12 month period. If this is not adhered to or there is insufficient resource to execute the requirements things will slip and the added pressure of leaving compliance monitoring to operate the business will fuel any critics and provide a negative effect on the firm's culture. Although we consider it to be an annual plan any timescale that works for your firm should be used.

If you have mapped your territory and your rules effectively alongside the financial products you will already have a very long list of things to check. Add to this the policies and procedures mentioned before and you will have no shortage of work to do. The annual training and competence plan should be kept as a separate part of your planning.

Your priorities will normally be set by the calendar, holiday periods and tax season but must be tempered with the current FCA hotspot, recent regulatory fines or other disciplinary actions and any changes to your business model. Deadlines must be set firmly but as with all planning an element of flexibility should be accepted. If you are fortunate to have staff assign responsibility accordingly. Allow some slack in your plan in case of requests from other department's advisers, March complaints or passed business reviews or whatever else may arise on an ad hoc basis. If you have multiple offices then repetition may be required but also bear in mind any budget that is set.

Risk management

If your firm is of a reasonable size, i.e. two or more RIs then it would be prudent to operate a risk management reporting tool of an appropriate scale. Within this tool should be sections reporting any regulatory training is due or has been completed as well as any regulatory remedial action plans for training and competence. Internal or external audit reports can also be reported here at a high level as well as overdue elements of your annual compliance monitoring plan.

In the risk identification section I prefer using a simple table covering the risk identified, Trigger, consequences if no action is taken, mitigating control, action plan, responsible, current and future risk rating, final date and current status. You can of course add anything further to this should you design but this often provide sufficient information for the directors to manage the company effectively.

If your firm is part of a group, or your firm is the parent of a group then you will obviously have a combination element to this information either to supply or collate on receipt. You should try to instil within the firm the belief that any risk is worth reporting even after an investigation may show that existing controls are sufficient. Nobody likes to shut the door after the horse has bolted.

Compliance advisory log

operating a compliance advisory log as previously mentioned also provide you with a form of analysis regarding consistent enquiries around certain areas, indicating potential training needs or flaws in current procedures or policies. These issues should be escalated as appropriate.

Regulatory contact log

The Compliance Manager should maintain a regulatory contact log similar to the compliance advisory log but based on external communication. All communication with the regulators should be coordinated through the Compliance Manager or compliance director and this log should be maintained with exact details of anything discussed or agreed.

Usually any contact with the regulator will be confirmed by them in an e-mail or letter, but it is good practice for you to do the same to confirm your understanding of what was discussed at any time.

Ensure that all staff are aware that any communication from the regulators should be passed through the Compliance Manager. There may be occasions where telephone calls are received from people purporting to be from the regulator and you should have within your policies details of how to address this eventuality. Members of the press have been known to elicit information from firms when no check to their validity has been made.

Complaint handling

Complaints are often a valuable source of information when the data is collated over time indicating potential weaknesses in your processes and procedures or training needs in the RIs. Complaints resolved by the end of the next working day need not be reported to the FCA but are a veritable goldmine of data for administration errors.

You should obviously have a written policy and procedure for handling complaints as well as a leaflet provided to eligible complainants which explains the process you will be following after the receipt of their complaint. It would be well to remember that all complaints should be treated seriously and that eligible complainants includes not only private individuals but small businesses some charities and trustees as well.

Training & Competency

The purpose of training and competence monitoring is to ensure that the staff are adequately trained the job they are expected to do. This complies with SYSC requirements for the competent employee rule which does not only include RIs. Although not specifically mentioned honesty should be considered as a function of competence along with the required skills, knowledge and expertise for a staff member to execute their responsibilities.

To comply with the competent employee rule most human resources best practice will already incorporate the required elements from conducting formal recruitment interviews, referencing, probationary period, job descriptions, appraisals, line manager and relevant training.

There must be a written policy for initial and ongoing maintenance of competence. If there are any regulatory changes that may impact on their work, arrangements must be available and known to accommodate these. Supervisors must insure they record the appropriate supervision methods and the results of monitoring before and after competence is obtained.

Should any adviser fail to achieve competence according to your T and C policy you are required to inform the FCA the reasons for this.

Approved Person Regime

It is the Compliance Manager's lot to maintain the AP log and ensure that all RI's are properly registered with the FCA or PRA. It is also your responsibility to ensure that all of the Controlled Function persons abide by the appropriate Approved Persons Code of Conduct (please note difference between PRA and FCA Code) and remain Fit & Proper.

Controlled functions are prescribed in Sup 10.4 and are divided into 5 functional areas;
- Governing Function
- Required Function
- The Systems & Control Function
- The Significant Management Function
- The Customer Function

The FCA have various forms in relation to the AP regime;
- Form A: application to perform a controlled function
- Form B: notice to withdraw an application to perform a controlled function
- Form C: notice of ceasing to perform a controlled function
- Form D: notice of change in the personal details of an approved person
- Form E: internal transfer of an approved person

These forms should be signed and vetted by compliance to ensure they been fully completed and reduce the risk of delay in processing. Before anyone becomes a member of staff in an approved person position you may wish to provide them with the FCA's fact sheet on "Becoming an Approved Person" and a copy of the statements of principle and also the code of practice for approved persons for which they will be expected to comply as well as summary details of their liability and the FCA is a disciplinary regime.

Management information

With the advent of the FCA's business risk awareness workshops in 2012, this highlights the need for good and accurate management information to be used in firms effectively. This enables senior management to understand what's going on in the firm so that they can deal with issues, identify trends and plan accordingly.

Since March 2008, when TCF measures required Management Information to provide a measure of how effective and the level of adherence of the application of the initiative, it seems that the FCA have increasingly encouraged businesses to use MI to demonstrate how they are operating and identify areas that may require some attention.

A recent survey of companies across the FCA spectrum has provided evidence that a number of firms use MI but few can explain what they use it for or why? Often these elements are forgotten over time and seldom reviewed to reflect contemporary needs or risk factors.

Designing MI to suit a company's needs is not always easy, as it takes some time in planning to identify exactly what is needed. While we can, and have helped a number of organisations of all sizes constructing MI, the bottom line is, as always, what is to be done with the data.

So why use MI or develop our own system for MI? Surely we know what is going on in our own business, don't we? Obviously we do, anecdotally and superficially that is clear, but how do we compare results to groups of people, processes or risks identified and, furthermore, identify trends and improving or deteriorating results over time? Even as that great fictional investigator of Agatha Christie fame, Hercule Poirot would remark, sometimes the little grey cells let us all down.

So if we are going to use any MI system, we have to understand and be absolutely clear on the form it is to take. There is no point in running multiple systems that offer a plethora of methods when all we will end up doing is getting confused: often challenging understanding about the definitions rather than the information.

Who does this apply to? Well, quite honestly everyone from sole trader to large concerns; no one is exempt.

Whilst a few people are afraid of doing things wrong by not having "the right" information it could easily be argued that, any information for comparison could be seen as better than none in many instances. Management information systems are designed to be organic and changeable over time, to develop with your business model, help you expand your business and can benefit you in many ways by assisting you to make better, informed decisions.

The basic rules needed for designing or improving any management information that we need is, to make it;

Relevant: Consider what is specifically relevant to your firm and who needs to see it or be aware of it.

Accurate: There is no point in making decisions based on rough figures or perceptions of performance.

Timely: How often does this need to be measured? Weekly; Monthly: Quarterly? Who needs to see it and when? Does it need to be collated first?

Acted upon: What are the key triggers? We know all about KPIs but what levels are acceptable? Be clear on what you are looking for and what you will do with it when you know.

Recorded: Write down in hard or soft copy what you do when you gather the information, why it is important and actions you will take at various thresholds or breaches. Circulate the results to those who need to know and incorporate any decisions in policy reviews.

The next item on your agenda has to be to decide how the information is going to be collected and used. How is it;

Gathered or sighted. New business register, Continuous Professional Development (CPD), Key Performance Indicators (KPIs), Key Risk Indicators (KRIs), training logs, compliance consultants reports, audits, TCF customer surveys, Not taken up (NTU) or Not proceeded with (NPW) applications, trail or legacy commissions, fees, training courses applied for or attended etc.

Analysis. How is this information collated? All information for everyone (name and shame) or certain data for Senior Management? Are there to be graphs, tables, bar charts or coloured segments to show progress, advancement on certain issues? Decide how you wish to present the information.

Circulation. Who needs to know and what level do they need to know? An adviser may need to know % of target for themselves and their team, but management may need to know lapse rate and case scores specifically.

Action. Hold regular 1:1 meeting with staff. Set trigger points and action plan frameworks to include remedial training or enhanced supervision.

Measurement. How are these elements to be measured and moved on? What trends are there; are tolerances being met? Do you need to use a scorecard?

Do not leave these fundamental steps to fall into place, because without them any further planning is unstable.

You have now decided what you are going to obtain MI on, and what you are going to do with it when you have got it, so now what?

Now you have to look at the business processes and decide what you consider relevant. To give you some ideas you could look at;

- Financial Position: Can you present to Senior Management that the company is meeting the FCA's own funds test and meet all liabilities as they fall due?

- Financial Rewards: Can you identify incentives or rewards that may encourage inappropriate behaviour amongst the management, staff or advisers?

- Span of Control: Do all individuals have the resources and adequate support to fulfil their role to the standards set by the company?

- Risk Management: Can you demonstrate that you have assessed and prioritised all risks and can evidence that risks are mitigated or accommodated accordingly as well as the culture displaying that TCF is fully embedded?

- Recruitment: Can you evidence that all Fit and Proper checks have been completed on all advisers and that previous complaints, concerns or other issues have had a satisfactory explanation or that periodic credit and other checks have provided comfort that there are no issues with advisers acting inappropriately?

- Competence and Qualification: Can you identify the gaps in adviser's knowledge and experience and take appropriate action to ensure any skill gaps are remedied or provided for? Can you confirm all advisers are adequately supervised?

- Turnover and retention: Can you confirm that the reasons for leaving are specifically individual and not endemic?

- Advice Process: Can you confirm that advisers are giving suitable advice and that their cases are being monitored adequately? How are the advisers risk rated? Do we know what sources of business are used by each adviser?

- Product/Provider Selection: Can you satisfy senior management that products are adequately recommended according to the client risk rating and that an appropriate range of products are considered for recommendation?

- Financial Promotions: Identify financial promotions campaigns and their link to profitability or additional business generation? Identify any root causes from complaints (either end of next working day or regulated, as applicable)?

- Complaints: Identify root causes and/or areas of concern for advisers or teams? Confirm all staff are aware of their responsibilities? Identify average time of complaints investigations and resolution?

Current Practices

How do you know if what you are doing is good or bad? Surely if it works for you, it is OK? It is your business after all.

The FCA have conducted studies of good and bad practices and while we are not going to provide each area duplicated in this document, we have reproduced some for you to get an idea of the things that are not bad practices, but could be better.

Good Practice

T&C

The T & C scheme included completing an initial risk assessment for each adviser by grading each of them. This would take into account industry experience, qualifications, complaints, types of business they would be writing, Key Performance Indicators (KPI's) and the results of file reviews. The three grades determined how much supervision each adviser needed.

Financial Promotions

The firm had a procedure in place that recorded customer queries and complaints received about their financial promotions. The results were measured and analysed enabling the firm to identify areas of concern and act upon them.

Poor Practice

The principal at the firm considered that because he trained and trusted an adviser, he didn't need to formally review his work. There was some form of training programme in place for a less experienced adviser. However, the lack of suitable monitoring and review procedures meant there was a real risk that customers could receive poorer quality of advice and the firm was exposed to the risk of future complaints.

The firm's website was not included in its 'Financial Promotions' checklist. Therefore, the firm did not remove out-of-date and inappropriate material from its website.

So to assess if your Management Information System is relevant, accurate, timely, acted upon and recorded, you will need to answer a number of questions. Here are some examples;

- Can you adequately assess the financial soundness of the people you recruit?
- Are new recruits adequately supervised?
- Can you identify weak areas of the advice process for individuals or a team?
- When was your Compliance Manual updated?
- Has the sales process changed since it was last documented?
- How well does your review service for clients work?
- Where there have been changes in circumstances for clients, do you review the previous advice?
- When were your processes last tested and checked?
- How do you measure your complaints; purely by numbers?
- Are you comfortable of the impact of your adviser's remuneration?

If you do not assess and measure your firm's recruitment procedures to ensure they are sufficiently robust, you could make inappropriate appointments. Identifying and addressing the root causes of staff turnover is good business practice. It could mean lower recruitment costs.

By identifying the level of competency of new advisers and understanding the type of business they will bring to your firm, you can assess if this is appropriate for the advice and services being provided to your customers and you can assess your firm's ability to adequately supervise them. This will reduce the risk of your firm giving customers poor advice.

Not assessing and measuring how your firm identifies gaps in adviser skills and knowledge or the quality of the training could lead to poor advice. Not measuring key indicators such as persistency rates, replacement business and complaints may hide issues which could develop into larger problems later.

These failures could lead to costly remedial action or regulatory discipline in the future.

So we have seen that assessing information gathered from key areas such as financial promotions, complaints, recruitment and training and competence, can help you measure the standards within your firm, identify risks, highlight where standards can be raised and helps to protect your business. These areas are high traffic areas and if you are involved in sales yourself, can be very demanding and detracting from your own business.

Areas that may be worthwhile reporting as management information are;

When you have agreed your key performance indicators (KPI) they will usually help form the management information you require. It is often best to check with the board or senior management what information they require that you have not yet captured. Frequency of reporting is vital in any modern business and the data may well need to be consolidated for less frequent but higher level meetings depending on the size of your business.

Chapter 17: AML activities

Anti-money-laundering and counterterrorist financing take-up a good part of the Compliance Manager's time. To ensure that the AML requirements are met your policies and procedures should be clear and unambiguous regarding is required. Too detail everything you need to cover would be overkill in the guidebooks such as this so we will cover the high-level points of various sections. It is important that you remember this guidance is provided as a summary only and you should tailor procedures and controls within your own firm to the requirements of your business model.

KYC approvals

The objective of this part is to ensure that no new clients business is transacted without evidence of their legal identity and residence being proven. Know your customer (KYC) is the term used for regulatory due diligence on new clients and is the fundamental frontline defence against money-laundering or terrorist financing.

The components of KYC are providing the customers identity ensuring that they resemble the picture identification obtained as well as evidence of their residence. KYC does not stop there as the very act of obtaining comfort about the customer's source of wealth, profession or activities, general bearing and reputation also add to the overall picture of the client as a potential investor. It is rare that anybody who is pretending to be reputable can maintain the facade when discussing their personal finances and personal plans.

KYC information is required before any business is transacted although there are certain exemptions in the money-laundering regulations 2007 paragraph 9.

Additional KYC requirements may be needed if the client is domiciled in another jurisdiction, the type of product recommended or needed require additional certification, the client pays acting for an unregulated charity or maybe classed as a politically exposed persons and you must have contingency plans to deal with these events depending on your business model.

If you are unable to complete KYC satisfactorily or to a level of comfort where you would be happy to deal with this person on behalf of your firm then the relationship should not be progressed and serious consideration should be made to reporting the situation as suspicious to the NCA.

You may decide that certain arrangements would be more suited for your business model such as;

- You risk rate your clients and below a certain risk level they are approved by office administrators and above this are submitted to compliance before any transactions are commenced.

- You may decide that the administrators can approve all new clients with occasional spot checks by compliance.

- That compliance approves all new clients.

- That one person in the administration is responsible for approving all new clients' KYC submissions.

Your database should be able to identify client's residence status or domicility and their nationality which may be important should any sanctions change or new legislation prohibits or permits certain transactions. Other information recorded on your customer relationship management would also be taken from the KYC and fact find information for marketing purposes.

Electronic KYC checking is more prevalent today and for a small cost you can check 99% of person's identity and residence saving a lot of time and money in shuffling paperwork. It is important to remember that not all providers will accept an electronic check as valid and your administrators should be made aware of those who will not accept.

Sanctions

Sanctions are imposed by HM Treasury, the EU commission and the United Nations by publishing lists of persons and entities which business should not be conducted with. The entries found on the sanctions lists were often contain the suspicions or findings against these persons and any nom de plume they may go under. In the UK a consolidated list is produced by HM Treasury for the use of individuals and businesses. The foreign and Commonwealth office and the Department for Business, Enterprise and Regulatory Reform (BERR) provide guidance in these matters.

You are required to conduct sanctions searches on new clients and whenever the sanctions list changes, which can be several times a week.

Although not covered by UK law the US sanctions regime under OFAC is particularly relevant if your firm or any part of the group in which you belong conduct business in US dollars as this places any transactions of this nature within the US sanctions regime extraterritorially.

Suspicions of money laundering

The procedures should be in place for identifying and processing any transactions where there are suspicions of money laundering or terrorist financing. You have a legal obligation to report suspicions of money laundering and terrorist financing to the NCA.

This area is critical in the U.K.'s fight against money-laundering and terrorist financing and you should ensure that you have conducted a full review of your firm is activities and client base. You should consider risk rating your client base using criteria that are appropriate such as location, level of income, amount of investable assets etc. and during this process identifying any weak spots in the recording of client data.

Procedures and regular training or refresher training should be implemented so that staff are aware constitutes a suspicious and a certain level of written reminder for them to refer to should be provided along with a pro forma reporting tool. This document should include;

- person reporting the suspicion
- date suspicion reported
- dates to which the suspicion relates
- nature of suspicion
- other persons concerned in the case
- client involved
- was legal advice considered/taken (details to be included)
- whether the report was forwarded to the NCA
- if so with what justification
- date suspicion considered closed (or reported to NCA)

Whenever a report is made the Compliance Manager should always investigate and if there is any foundation to the suspicion a report to NCA should be made. NCA issues guidance about procedures to be followed in relation to reports of suspicions and these should be followed to the letter in order to avoid legal actions in the future. Tipping off is a very real occurrence and thereby procedures supplied should be followed to the letter.

KYC reviews

With the legislation published in 2007 and the guidance from the JMLSG, ongoing reviews of clients are required to ensure their details are up-to-date.

The individual profile of a client may well change and evolve over time and it's important that these changes are captured in the firm's records. If annual reviews are conducted and fact find is are completed at set periods it is important to ensure that these details are refreshed in the customer relationship management tool or database.

Typically the things that will change our marital status, company ownership or directorships, name changes, inheritances and frequency of transactions, children, promotions etc. by keeping these details up-to-date you can honestly say that you continue to KYC.

Third-party introductions

Third-party introductions present KYC issues and you should ensure there are suitable controls around accepting any introductions or referrals from third parties. There are certain circumstances by which you can rely on other bodies to have completed KYC on a client but you should still be comfortable that the KYC conducted has been adequate.

The Applicable AML regulations are detailed in Appendix 1

Chapter 18: Compliance with Senior Management

In this chapter I will provide a brief description of the areas that you should consider as part of compliance responsibilities and where necessary at insufficient comment to explain the stance.

As we have previously established senior management are responsible for the governance of firms in their charge and they are responsible for setting strategy and implementing their decisions, reviewing performance of the firm, setting remuneration policy; reporting to shareholders and other stakeholders; setting the management structure and reporting lines and delegating the authority to staff members; receiving, reviewing and acting on management information from the operational side of the business; monitoring risk and addressing problems, and of course, are responsible for compliance.

There are a number of regulatory areas which are particularly relevant to senior management and we have covered most of those areas in previous text. There are other areas within the firm that have regulatory responsibilities or are impacted by regulatory regime and these would be the human resources, marketing, IT, company secretary, legal and risk, finance, audit and administration. Specific regulatory relevance will depend on your business model and the size of your company and to list all potential regulatory impacts would in most cases be pointless.

Appendices

Appendix 1: Applicable AML Regulations

The impacts of these various pieces of legislation may not directly impact on all sized firms, but it is always useful to be aware of them in case of future developments and especially if dealing with corporates or HNW clients that have overseas interests. A brief explanation follows. The key sections of this Order that are of relevance to financial services firms are noted below. ***Only those of particular relevance to financial services firms are covered***

1. ***The Anti-Terrorism, Crime and Security Act 2001***

   Overview

   ATCSA strengthens the UK government's powers to combat terrorism, as previously

   Set out in the Terrorism Act 2000 (TACT) (see page 14), and it amends TACT in number of areas. One particular addition of note is the arrangements in sections 17 – 20 (see below)

   Designed to strengthen both the national and international anti-terrorist network. ATCSA is not aimed only at combating terrorism and also has provisions relating to other areas relevant to crime and security such as bribery, corruption and actions likely to have a detrimental effect on the UK economy.

   Main elements

   Firms should have systems and controls in place to ensure compliance with ATCSA;

   – a failure to do so could result in a criminal offence, regulatory breaches and sanctions, and serious loss of reputation.

For further guidance on controls relating to money laundering and terrorist financing see Appendix B of the main text.

Key Sections

1   Gives effect to Schedule 1 of ATCSA which relates to the forfeiture of terrorist funds and property. Repeals sections 24–31 of TACT. Refers to Schedule 2 which amends the definition of terrorist property as initially set out in TACT.

4 - 16   Sets out procedures relating to the freezing orders that may be made if the UK Treasury reasonably believes that action is likely to take place to the detriment of the UK economy or which is likely to constitute a threat to the life or property of a UK national or resident.

17 – 20 Provisions relating to the disclosure by public authorities (as defined under the Human Rights Act – see Appendix 3) of information relating to criminal investigations and proceedings to other authorities in the UK and overseas.

102 – 107 Provisions relating to the retention of communications data that could have an impact on a firm's record-keeping arrangements.

108 - 110 Establishes the extra territorial reach of the UK's bribery and corruption offences as set out in the:
- Prevention of Corruption Act 1906;
- Public Bodies Corrupt Practices Act 1889; and
- Prevention of Corruption Act 1916.

117   amends section 38 of TACT with the addition of section 38B which makes it an offence to fail to

report information that could help to prevent terrorism.

Schedule 1   Arrangements relating to the forfeiture of terrorist cash and the handling and tracing of terrorist property. Includes a definition of terrorist cash and property. Amended slightly by section 35 of TACT 06.

Schedule 2 (part I)   Amends section 38 of TACT with the addition of section 38A which gives effect to the new Schedule 6A concerning account monitoring orders.

Schedule 2 (part II)   Amends Schedule 4 of TACT relating to forfeiture orders.

Schedule 2 (part III)   Amends section 21 of TACT with the addition of sections 21A, 21B. Amends Schedule 3 of TACT with the addition of Schedule 3A.

Schedule 2 (part IV)   Amends Schedule 6 of TACT

Schedule 3   additional details on freezing orders which may be implemented if the UK Treasury reasonably believes that action is likely to take place to the detriment of the UK economy or which is likely to constitute a threat to the life or property of a UK national or resident. Establishes offences relating to non-compliance with freezing orders. These offences may also be attributable to officers of bodies corporate, for example, directors and managers.

2. The Money Laundering Regulations 2007

Overview

Legislation setting out the legal obligations of 'relevant businesses' (as defined by the

ML Regulations and including financial services firms) to identify their customers and generally help prevent money laundering.

Main elements

The regulations set out the detailed requirements that regulated firms must comply with, in order to meet their statutory obligations to prevent money laundering.

The ML Regulations form one of the core documents upon which the Joint Money Laundering Steering Group Guidance Notes are based.

Key Sections

2	*Contains many useful definitions required for a full understanding of the ML Regs.*
3	*Lists the persons to whom the ML Regs apply.*
4	*Lists the persons to whom the ML Regs do not apply. For further guidance see Schedule 2.*
5	*Defines the term 'customer due diligence'.*
6	*Defines the term 'beneficial owner' for the purposes of completing customer due diligence.*
7	*Establishes when customer due diligence should be completed. Indicates that a risk-based approach to customer due diligence should be implemented.*
8	*Indicates that business relationships should be subject to ongoing monitoring in terms of keeping customer due diligence information up to date.*

9	Establishes that the identity of the customer and the beneficial owner must be verified before the establishment of a business relationship or the carrying out of an occasional transaction.
11	Requires business to cease if it is not possible to complete satisfactory due diligence. · Indicates that if it is not possible to complete due diligence then consideration should be given to whether a disclosure should be made under Part 7 of the Proceeds of Crime Act 2002 or Part 3 of the Terrorism Act 2000.
12	Exempts trustees of debt issues from the requirement to complete due diligence on the holders of the investments that fall within articles 77 and 78 of the Regulated Activities Order. Such relevant investments include corporate and government debt instruments.
13	Establishes the instances in which simplified due diligence may be completed.
14	Sets out when enhanced due diligence and ongoing monitoring arrangements should be implemented, such as with politically exposed persons.
15	Indicates that controls at least as strict as those established by the ML Regs should be implemented by branches and subsidiaries outside the EEA (those within the EEA will also be subject to the EU's money-laundering legislation on which the ML Regs are based).
16	Prohibits firms from entering into, or continuing, a correspondent banking relationship with a shell bank. Prohibits firms from operating anonymous accounts.

17	*Establishes the basis upon which a firm may rely on a third party for due diligence purposes.*
18	*Powers of the Treasury in relation to persons against whom the Financial Action Task Force has applied counter measures.*
19	*Establishes due diligence record-keeping requirements in terms of content and retention period.*
20	*Requires firms to implement risk-based policies and procedures to prevent money laundering and terrorist financing. These policies and procedures should cover:* • *customer due diligence requirements and ongoing monitoring arrangements;* • *reporting;* • *record keeping;* • *internal controls;* • *risk assessment and management; and* • *the administration of such policies and procedures.*
21	*Imposes the requirement of firms to train their employees in relation to the prevention of money laundering and terrorist financing.*
23	*Establishes various supervisory bodies, including the FCA, for the purposes of anti-money laundering and terrorist financing prevention.*
24	*Establishes the duties of supervisory authorities.*
37	*Establishes the right of the FCA and other anti-money laundering authorities to obtain information from firms and their employees, as well as to arrange interviews and view recorded*

information, for the purposes of enforcing the ML Regs.

3. The Proceeds of Crime Act 2002

Overview

POCA focuses on preventing criminals from benefiting from their crimes by enhancing the ability of law enforcement agencies to seize criminal funds.

Main elements

Establishes a number of offences of which financial services firms may find themselves guilty if they fail to implement adequate money laundering arrangements. Describes how firms may be required to cooperate during the course of an investigation under POCA.

Key Sections

1 - 5   Create the Asset Recover Agency (ARA) which is a body empowered to recover profit derived from criminal activity. (Note that ARA was incorporated into the Serious and Organised Crime Agency (SOCA) and is now part of the NCA).

6 - 316 Set out the legal framework within which criminal proceeds may be confiscated.

241   Establishes that conduct undertaken overseas, that would constitute a criminal offence if undertaken in any part of the UK, is deemed to be unlawful conduct for the purposes of POCA.

327   Makes it an offence to conceal criminal property. Clarifies that the concept of concealing criminal property is very wide and includes the actions of disguising its nature, source, location, disposition, movement or ownership or any rights with respect to it. There are certain exemptions to this offence

including having reported the relevant circumstances in accordance with section 338 of POCA and having received the appropriate consent under section 335 of POCA.

328   Makes it an offence for a person to enter into or become involved with an arrangement which he knows or suspects facilitates the acquisition, use, retention or control of criminal property by or on behalf of another. There are certain exemptions to this offence, including having reported the relevant circumstances in accordance with section 338 of POCA and having received the appropriate consent under section 335 of POCA.

329   Makes it an offence to acquire, use or possess criminal property. · There are certain exemptions to this offence, including having reported the relevant circumstances in accordance with section 338 of POCA and having received the appropriate consent under section 335 of POCA.

330   Makes it an offence to fail to report knowledge or a suspicion of money laundering if the following three conditions are met:
- the person has knowledge or suspects that another person is engaged in money laundering.
- the person concerned gained their knowledge or suspicion as a result of their work for a regulated firm.
- the person did not make a report of their suspicion to their firm's MLRO (or other internally nominated person) or to another person authorized for this purpose.

There are certain exemptions to this offence – notably the fact that the person did not receive anti-money laundering training from his employer.

In considering whether an offence has been committed under this section the court will consider whether the person complied with relevant guidance such as the JMLSG Guidance Notes.

331 Makes it an offence for a nominated officer, such as an MLRO, to fail to report a suspicion of money laundering that they have received under section 330 above if three conditions are met:
- the nominated officer has knowledge or suspects that another person is engaged in money laundering.

- the person concerned gained their knowledge or suspicion as a result of a disclosure made under section 330 above.

- the person did not make a report of their suspicion to a person nominated for this purpose by SOCA (now NCA).

Failure to report is not an offence if there is an explanation for the fact that a report was not made. In considering whether an offence has been committed under this section the court will consider whether the nominated officer complied with relevant guidance such as the JMLSG Guidance Notes.

333 Establishes the offence of tipping off. The offence of tipping off is committed if a person knows or suspects that a disclosure has been made under sections 337 or 338 above and he discloses this fact in such a way that is likely to jeopardize any

resultant investigation. There are certain limited exemptions.

334   Sets out the penalties for offences created under sections 327–333 (see below). 335 Defines 'appropriate consent' for the purposes of the exemptions to the offences described at sections 327–329 of POCA.

336   Sets out the circumstances in which those authorized to give 'appropriate consent' may do so. If consent is given in breach of this section an offence is committed.

337   Defines the term 'protected disclosures'. A person may lawfully disclose a suspicion or knowledge of money laundering (where otherwise disclosing the information would have been an offence), as long as the disclosure meets certain conditions including that of having been made to a constable, a customs officer or a nominated officer such as the person's MLRO. 338 Defines the term 'authorized disclosure' for the purposes of the exemptions to the offences described at sections 327–329 of POCA.

339   Sets out requirements relating to the form and manner of disclosures as per sections 330,

331, 332 and 338 of POCA.

340   Clarifies the meaning of certain terms used in POCA including those described below. Establishes that 'criminal conduct' includes conduct undertaken overseas that would constitute a criminal offence if undertaken in any part of the UK. Defines the term 'criminal property' for the purposes of POCA. Property is defined very broadly and includes money and all forms of property, real or personal, heritable or moveable,

or intangible. Provides the following definition of money laundering:
- an act which:

- constitutes an offence under section 327, 328 or 329 of POCA;

- constitutes an attempt, conspiracy or incitement to commit an offence

- specified in paragraph (a);

- constitutes aiding, abetting, counselling or procuring the commission of an

- offence specified in paragraph (a); or

- would constitute an offence specified in paragraph (a), (b) or (c) if done in the United Kingdom.

Defines the terms 'constable' and 'nominated officer'.

341 Describes the various types of investigation that may take place under POCA including money-laundering investigations.

342 Makes it an offence (with certain exemptions) to prejudice an investigation under POCA.

345-346 Describe arrangements relating to production orders that may be made during an investigation under POCA.

347 Indicates that production orders may authorize entry to premises during the course of an investigation under POCA.

352 - 356 Set out arrangements in relation to search and seizure warrants that may be issued during the course of an investigation under POCA.

357-362 Set out arrangements in relation to disclosure orders that may be issued during the course of an investigation under POCA.

359 Set out the offences that may be committed in relation to disclosure orders.

363-369 Establish that financial services firms may be subject to customer information orders under POCA. Describe arrangements in relation to such customer information orders. Customer information orders require firms to disclose certain key pieces of information about a customer including:
- account number;
- full name;
- date of birth;
- evidence of identity obtained by the firm; and
- tax number.

366 Sets out the offences that may be committed in relation to customer information orders (see below).

370-376 Establish that financial services firms may be required to comply with account monitoring orders under POCA.

Describe arrangements in relation to such account monitoring orders.

Account monitoring orders require firms to provide account information to a particular law enforcement agency if certain illegal activity, including money laundering, is suspected.

There are special arrangements for making account monitoring orders relating to information held overseas.

Sch 1 Describes arrangements for the operation of the Assets Recovery Agency

Sch 2, 4 & 5 List the offences known as 'lifestyle' offences in England and Wales, Scotland and Northern Ireland respectively.

Lifestyle offences are those that would tend to indicate that a person has a 'criminal lifestyle' and may therefore be subject to the assets confiscation regime under POCA.

4. **The Serious Organised Crime and Police Act 2005**

Overview

Law designed to strengthen the powers of the police to combat serious, organised crime.

Main elements

NCA replaces SOCA, the body previously responsible for receiving notifications of suspicions of money laundering with a new agency called the National Crime Agency (NCA). Firms must comply with the detailed requirements of NCA when dealing with a suspicion of money laundering. Financial services firms may be required to provide information or documents under a disclosure order to assist with a criminal investigation. Firms or individuals convicted of certain offences may find themselves subject to a financial reporting order. NCA amends certain key sections of POCA.

Key Sections

1-59 These sections establish the responsibilities, powers and general modus operandi of NCA.

60-65   Confer powers on relevant investigating authorities to make disclosure notices in relation to certain crimes.

The investigating authorities referenced are the:
- Director of Public Prosecutions;
- Director of Revenue and Customs Prosecutions;
- Lord Advocate.
- The crimes covered include:
- drug trafficking;
- money laundering;
- engaging in terrorist activities.
- Disclosure notices can be made by:
- a police constable;
- an appropriately designated member of NCA; or
- an officer of Revenue and Customs.

Disclosure notices are designed to assist with investigations into crime and require persons on whom an order has been made to provide information and/or documents in accordance with the time and place requirements stipulated by the relevant investigating authority.

66   Establishes the power of the authorities to seize documents subject to a disclosure notice under warrant if these have not been produced as required.

67   Failure to comply with a disclosure notice may constitute an offence (see below).

68-70 Various other matters relating to disclosure notices, including the ways in which disclosure notices may be given.

76-81 Financial reporting orders may be made on persons found guilty of certain crimes such as:
- drug trafficking;
- money laundering;
- engaging in terrorist activities.

Financial reporting orders require the subject to disclose details of their financial affairs and supply supporting documentation. Failure to comply with a financial reporting order constitutes an offence.

95 -96 Provision relating to the strengthening of international cooperation in fighting crime.

97–109 Various amendments to POCA, including (at section 102) the removal of the troublesome Spanish bullfighter problem).

Schedules 1-4 Matters relating to the operation of NCA.

5. **The Terrorism Act 2000 (as amended by the Anti-Terrorism, Crime and Security Act 2001).**

Overview

TACT defines terrorism for the purposes of the UK legal system and creates the legal powers necessary to combat it.

It is the UK's primary counter-terrorism legislation.

TACT creates a number of offences related to involvement in arrangements for facilitating, raising or using funds for terrorist purposes. Specifically, it is an offence:

- Not to report a suspicion of terrorist activity where there are reasonable grounds to suspect this; and
- To take action that is likely to 'tip off' a person who is suspected of involvement in terrorism.

TACT gives law enforcement agencies the power to make account monitoring orders, similar to those introduced by POCA if it is suspected that a particular client account is being used for terrorist purposes.

TACT also lists organizations that have been proscribed, and with which firms should not consequently conduct business.

Main elements

TACT makes it an offence to facilitate terrorism in any way and as a consequence financial services firms must make sure that they have the appropriate systems and controls in place to ensure that they are not unwittingly used for this purpose.

Key Sections

1	Provides a definition of terrorism for the purposes of TACT. Amended slightly by section 34 of TACT 06.
3-13	Matters relating to proscribed organizations (suspected of involvement with terrorism). Amended by sections 21 and 22 of TACT 06 to have a more extensive reach.
14	Provides a definition of terrorist property for the purposes of TACT. This has been amended by Schedule 2 of the ATCSA.
15	Creates the offence of terrorist fund raising – see below.

16   Creates the offence of use and possession of terrorist money or property – see below.

17 & 18 Create the offence of being involved in terrorist funding arrangements – see below.

19 & 20 Creates the requirement to report a suspicion of an offence having been committed under sections 15–18 of TACT. Require such reports to be made as soon as is reasonably practical to either a constable or to an appropriately nominated person (such as the MLRO) within a financial services firm.

The duty to report only applies when a person forms a suspicion on the basis of their involvement with their trade, profession, business or employment. (By way of example, if you are travelling on public transport and suspect that a fellow passenger is carrying a bomb then you are under no legal duty to report this. However, if you are at work in a bank and suspect that one of your customers is using their account to fund terrorist activities, you have a duty to report it.)

21   Provides that it is not an offence for a person to continue their involvement with a constable (or to the relevant internal person such as the MLRO) and the constable has not forbidden their continuing involvement.

21A   Addition to TACT created under the ATCSA. Creates an offence specifically covering persons working within the regulated sector for failure to report a suspicion of terrorism.

21B   Addition to TACT created under the ATCSA. Establishes 'protected disclosure' requirements specifically for the regulated sector whereby an employee of a regulated sector firm may report a suspicion of terrorist activity to a constable or to a 'nominated officer' appointed by their employer.

22   Sets out the penalties for an offence under sections 15 – 18 of TACT – see below.

24-31   These sections previously set out the powers of forfeiture created under TACT in relation to money or property belonging to a person convicted under sections 15 – 18. However, they have ceased to have effect under section 1.4 of the ATCSA.

37   Gives effect to Schedule 5 of TACT which sets out the powers of a constable to search premises and seize material as part of a terrorist investigation. Amended and strengthened by section 26 of TACT 06.

38   Gives effect to Schedule 6 of TACT which sets out the powers of a constable to obtain financial information about the clients of a financial institution. Such information includes evidence of a person's identity obtained for KYC purposes and the date on which the relationship with the financial institution began or ended.

38A   Addition to TACT created under the ATCSA. Gives effect to the new Schedule 6A concerning account monitoring orders.

38B   Addition to TACT created under the ATCSA. Makes it an offence to fail to disclose certain information about terrorism.

39   Creates the offences of 'tipping off' a person subject to a terrorist investigation and/or interfering with material likely to be relevant to such an investigation.

63	Establishes the extraterritorial reach of TACT by stating that if an act constituting an offence under TACT is committed outside the UK, the person who commits it shall still be deemed to have committed an offence for the purposes of TACT.
64	Amends the Extradition Act 1989 to cover offences under sections 15 – 18 of TACT (now repealed and incorporated into the Extradition Act 2003).
Schedule 2	Lists the organizations proscribed under TACT.
Schedule 3A	Addition to TACT created under the ATCSA. Defines regulated sector businesses and supervisory authorities (including the *FCA*) for the purposes of TACT.
Schedule 4	Procedures and arrangements relating to forfeiture orders made under TACT. Amended by the ATCSA.
Schedule 5	See section 37 above – terrorist investigations.
Schedule 6	See section 38 above – provision of financial information during the course of an investigation into terrorism. Amended by Schedule 2 Part IV of the ATCSA.
Schedule 6A	Addition to TACT created under the ATCSA. Procedures relating to Account Monitoring Orders which may be made specifically against financial services institutions for the purposes of tracing suspected terrorist cash property.

6. **The Terrorism Act 2006**

Overview

Enacted in order to further strengthen the government's powers to combat the threat of international terrorism.

Main elements

See comments for previous section - TACT 00.

Key Sections

21 Amends section 3 of TACT 00 to increase the scope of activities that may lead to an organization being proscribed.

22 Amends section 3 of TACT 00 to cover name changes of proscribed organizations.

26 Amends Schedule 5 Part I of TACT 00 to increase powers relating to searches for the purposes of terrorist investigations.

34 Slight amendment to the definition of terrorism set out in section 1 of TACT 00.

35 Slight amendment to Schedule 1 of the ATCSA concerning the amount of time that seized terrorist cash may be held.

7. **The Terrorism (United Nations Measures) Order 2006**

Overview

Prohibits terrorist financing and the provision of financial services to terrorists.

Allows the Treasury to freeze the funds/ accounts of suspected terrorists.

Main elements

The asset freezing provisions introduced under the Terrorism Order may result in liquidity problems – assets that are due to be paid to a third party may be frozen and consequently, additional funds will need to be made available to meet the delivery obligations.

Firms that do not have adequate controls in place to counter their being used to provide financial services to terrorists may find themselves guilty of an offence under the Terrorism Order.

Key Sections

2   Provides definition for key terms used in the Terrorism Order.

3 & 4   Relate to the designation of individuals for the purposes of this Order. A person may be designated either by a decision of the EU Council or by a direction of the UK Treasury. The Treasury may designate persons in a number of circumstances – if it suspects that a person is:
- involved with terrorism;
- subject to an EU Council decision relating to this area;
- owned or controlled, either directly or indirectly, by a designated person;
- acting on behalf of a designated person.

5   Requires the Treasury, among other things, to publicize its decision to designate a person under this Order.

6   Makes it an offence to disclose information about the Treasury's decision to designate a person under this Order where this information has only been made available to certain persons.

7   Makes it an offence for a person to deal with funds or other economic resources belonging to a person designated under this Order. Accounts in which such funds or economic resources are held are

deemed 'frozen accounts' for the purposes of this Order. For the purposes of this Order, the definition of 'to deal with' is very wide and covers most if not all involvement that a financial services firm could have with a designated person. A person may only deal with such funds legal under the authority of a licence issued by the Treasury under article 11 of this Order.

8 Makes it an offence to make funds, economic resources or financial services available, directly or indirectly, to or for the benefit of a person designated under this order. The restrictions in this section may only be lawfully breached with the authority of licence issued by the Treasury under article 11 of this Order.

10 Makes it an offence to breach, or assist another person in breaching, requirements under sections 7 and 8 of this Order.

11 Covers the Treasury's authority to grant a licence for lawfully engaging in activities that would otherwise be illegal under sections 7 and 8 of this Order.

13 Sets out the penalties that may be imposed for breaching this Order. Provides that where a body corporate has been found guilty of an offence under this Order, then its directors, managers and other staff may also be guilty of an offence.

Schedule 1.1 Requires the Treasury to cooperate fully with any national or international investigation regarding a person designated under this Order.

Schedule 1.2 Makes it an offence for a financial institution to fail to inform the Treasury of knowledge or a suspicion that a designated person has committed an offence under sections 6, 7, 8, 10 or 11 of this Order where that person is or has been a customer of the firm, or the firm has otherwise had involvement with them, since the implementation of the Terrorism (United Nations Measures) Order 2001.

Schedule 1.3   Gives authority to the Treasury to require information and documents to be made available to it in cases in which terrorism is suspected.

Schedule 1.4   Sets out the penalties for failing to provide information to the Treasury during a terrorism investigation and for failing to cooperate with Treasury investigations into terrorism.

8. **Trade and Financial Sanctions Legislation**

Overview

Trade and financial sanctions legislation is aimed at preventing the UK's financial system from being used by criminal or corrupt regimes, organizations or persons or for facilitating undesirable activities such as terrorism and arms dealing. The regime is the overall responsibility of the Foreign and Commonwealth Office with the financial sanctions regime being operated by the Asset Freezing Unit of HM Treasury and the trade sanctions regime being operated by the Department for Business, Enterprise and Regulatory Reform.

New sanctions are accompanied by a statutory instrument so that they are legally enforceable and details are published on the Treasury's website. This should be checked regularly by Compliance as firms must not conduct any trades in breach of financial sanctions legislation.

Examples of statutory instruments implementing a sanction
- The Al-Qa'ida and Taliban (United Nations Measures) Order 2006 (see page 2).
- The Burma (Financial Sanctions) Regulations 2005.
- The Export Control (Democratic Republic of Congo) Order 2005.
- The Federal Republic of Yugoslavia (Freezing of Funds) (Amendment) Regulations 2001.
- The International Criminal Tribunal for the Former Yugoslavia (Financial Sanctions Against Indictees) Regulations 2005.
- United Nations Security Council Resolution 1747 (2007).
- The Iraq (United Nations Sanctions) Order 2000 (Amendment No. 2) Regulations 2004.
- The Ivory Coast (United Nations Sanctions) Order 2005
- United Nations Security Council Resolution 1973 (2011)
- United Nations Security Council Resolution 1989 (2011)

Appendix 2: Bribery Act 2010

Many authorised firms are still wondering about the best way to implement the Bribery Act and what it means to them as a business and a trading company that uses and provides corporate entertainment. Though mostly common sense and good business practice, whenever a legislative wrapper is placed around guidance, people are wary of not falling foul of the new law.

Our aim is to provide you with a brief insight into what can be a complex area, and give you contact details of specialists who can help and assist you with your strategy, governance and operational needs.

Introduction

Now part of British Law, the *Bribery Act 2010* (The Act) reforms criminal law to provide a new, modern and comprehensive scheme of bribery offences as never before understood, that will enable courts and prosecutors to respond more effectively to bribery at home or abroad.

The Act applies to all persons individual and corporate making it an offence to; a) Bribe another person; or b) to be in receipt of a bribe from another person.

The Scope of the Act

The Act deals with bribery which is defined as giving someone a financial or other advantage to encourage that person to perform their function or activities improperly, or to reward that person for having already done so. Surprisingly for some, The Act is not concerned with other offences such as fraud, theft or offences under the Companies Acts, but anyone who facilitates the movement of the proceeds of bribery also commits money laundering offences.

How could my company become liable?

Your company could become liable very easily through lack of systems and controls to prevent bribery or insufficient checks to ensure that it has not occurred. Commercial companies that seek to generate new business or maintain an existing business channel, domestic or foreign, is faced with a hugely competitive environment, and the people who are in a position to grant valuable business contracts often realise that they are in a position to demand significant benefits or favours from anybody seeking their business.

Over many years, the practice of bribing people in influential positions becomes such a well-practiced habit that in so many areas it is hardly considered to be unusual. Many companies that conduct business in these areas have become used to building such up-front costs into their tendering processes.

However, if a responsible officer of your company commits such an offence now, or they knowingly allow it to carry on, then a bribery offence is committed, and the criminal acts will be attributed to the company. The liability is fully extended to any situation where <u>an agent</u>, <u>employee</u> or <u>intermediary</u> pays a bribe to get business, keep business or obtain a business advantage.

If your company has failed to take the necessary steps to implement adequate procedures to prevent bribery, you will be liable for their actions.

Additionally, under FSMA section 206(1) *"If the FCA considers that an authorised person has contravened a requirement imposed on him by or under this Act … it may impose on him a penalty, in respect of the contravention, of such amount as it considers appropriate"* and the firm can be fined for breaches of Principle 3 of the *FCA's* Principles for Businesses; *"A firm must take reasonable care to organise and control its affairs responsibly and effectively, with adequate risk management systems"* and Rule SYSC 3.2.6 R of the FCA's Senior Management Arrangements, Systems and Controls Handbook *"A firm must take reasonable care to establish and maintain effective systems and controls for compliance with applicable requirements and standards under the regulatory system and for countering the risk that the firm might be used to further financial crime.". SYSC 4.1.1R (For Common Platform Firms) states "A firm must have robust governance arrangements, which include a clear organisational structure with well defined, transparent and consistent lines of responsibility, effective processes to identify, manage, monitor and report the risks it is or might be exposed to, and internal control mechanisms, including sound administrative and accounting procedures and effective control and safeguard arrangements for information processing systems"*

How do I implement sufficiently adequate procedures?

Initially you need to accurately assess what bribery risks you might face. If you are a UK financial services company you have probably already undertaken a Risk Based Assessment (RBA), as part of your compliance process, but if you are a commercial organisation, you may not have undertaken such an exercise and could find that you need professional assistance to construct an accurate assessment!

Having accurately conducted your RBA, you need to consider the following elements to create an effective compliance regime to prevent bribery.

- Proportionality:
- High-Level Commitment:
- Risk Assessment:
- Due Diligence:
- Internal Communication:
- Regular Monitoring and Review

Two Most Asked Questions;

Can I still provide hospitality? Can I make facilitation payments?

Yes, you can still provide business hospitality, as long as it is reasonable and proportionate in all the circumstances. As the Justice Minister, Kenneth Clark has said;

'... Taking customers to Twickenham is normal...but if you took them for a Caribbean cruise with their wife, that's different. It is normal business hospitality to get to know your customers better. No one is going to call that dishonest...'

However, in too many circumstances, the demands of hospitality have become a cover-all for expenditure that reaches such a volume that it cannot be described as anything other than a bribe, and it is this degree of proportionality which will be measured in the future.

Secondly; No, facilitation payments will not be permitted. Unlike the US law, such payments are still defined as bribes in UK law and will be dealt with as such.

What should I be doing to ensure that I am fully compliant with the law?

You must complete a full review of your business risk areas and establish where you believe you are at the greatest risk from bribery. Then, with this knowledge and having established your full RBA, you should implement a full compliance review, with a view to introducing a compliance policy document and implementing your internal training needs. This will then protect you from internal or external allegations that you have been negligent in preventing bribery in your organisation.

How can we help you?

Ensuring your firm is prepared for every variable takes expertise and guidance. Compliance Consultant will help you manage your risks, strengthen your compliance programme, and achieve transparency and control to meet and surpass the requirements of the *Bribery Act 2010*.

Protecting your firm and building effective systems and controls requires risk specialists with a deep understanding of the issues you are facing. In addition, our consultants can assist you in delivering your programme to your directors, staff and agents –

this can also include your contractors and suppliers if this is appropriate.

Contact us today and let our experts demonstrate their knowledge and skills to drive your regulatory processes by providing you with a review of your current anti-bribery policies.

info@complianceconsultant.org

Appendix 3: Bibliographies

These Bibliographies are designed to aid your navigation for the required rules and guidance and in no way form a recommendation or direction for use. The references to the rules and FCA handbook or other sections have been fully checked and updated as of April 2013.

To access the FCA handbook and its constituent sourcebooks:
http://fshandbook.info/FS/html/FCA

The new PRA Handbook can be found at
http://www.bankofengland.co.uk/pra/Pages/default.aspx

Bibliographies Sections

Compliance Oversight & the Compliance Function

Conduct of Business and Client Assets

Regulatory Approach to Risk Management

Compliance & Ethics

Anti-Money Laundering

PRA Links

Compliance Oversight and the Compliance Function

	Subject matter	Source material
1	The role of the FCA in consumer protection	Essential facts about the FCA http://www.fca.org.uk/about/what FCA - What we do http://www.fca.org.uk/about/why-we-do-it How we are governed http://www.fca.org.uk/about/governance Doing business with the FCA http://www.fca.org.uk/about/what How we are funded http://www.fca.org.uk/about/how-we-are-funded Our Structure http://www.fca.org.uk/about/structure
2	How firms are authorised to undertake regulated activities	Firm Types http://www.fca.org.uk/firms/firm-types About Authorisation http://www.fca.org.uk/firms/about-authorisation Being regulated http://www.fca.org.uk/firms/being-regulated Markets http://www.fca.org.uk/firms/markets COND – Threshold Conditions http://fshandbook.info/FS/html/FCA/COND PERG – Perimeter Guidance http://fshandbook.info/FS/html/FCA/PERG Financial Services Products

		http://www.fca.org.uk/firms/financial-services-products
3	The regulatory implications of appointing an agent (including appointed representatives and outsourcing)	SUP – Supervision http://fshandbook.info/FS/html/FCA/SUP SYSC – Organisation; Employees and Agents http://fshandbook.info/FS/html/FCA/SYSC/5
4	How the FCA supervises firms and individuals	SUP – Supervision http://fshandbook.info/FS/html/FCA/SUP FIT – The fit and proper test for approved persons http://fshandbook.info/FS/html/FCA/FIT APER - Statements of Principle & Code of Practice for Approved Persons http://fshandbook.info/FS/html/FCA/APER
5	How and in what circumstances the FCA exercises its enforcement and disciplinary powers.	The Enforcement Guide http://fshandbook.info/FS/html/FCA/EG
6	The FCA decision making procedures	Decision Procedure and Penalties Manual http://fshandbook.info/FS/html/FCA/DEPP
7	The role of the compliance function within a firm's risk management framework	"Financial Services Authority Regulation and Risk-based Compliance", by Stuart Bazley and Dr. Andrew Haynes (Tottel publishing).
8	How the use of	"Essential Strategies for Financial Services

198

	agents impacts on a firm's risk profile	Compliance" by Annie Mills.
9	The impact of an effective compliance function on the firm's compliance standards and culture	"Handbook of Compliance", by Andrew Newton (published by Global Knowledge Solutions)
10	Compliance requirements and standards, and their implications for the firm	
11	How effective compliance policies, plans and oversight can mitigate regulatory risks in the business	
12	How to establish and manage a constructive regulatory relationship.	Financial Services Authority Regulation and Risk-based Compliance (Chapter 11), by Stuart Bazley & Dr. Andrew Haynes (Tottel publishing).

Conduct of Business and Client Assets

	Subject matter	Source material
1	The general application and scope of the Conduct of Business and Client Assets rules	COBS and CASS Activities, scope and purpose http://fshandbook.info/FS/html/FCA/COBS http://fshandbook.info/FS/html/FCA/CASS/1 http://fshandbook.info/FS/html/FCA/CASS/1A Source EU Markets in Financial Instruments Directive (MiFID) for conduct of business matters http://eur-lex.europa.eu/LexUriServ/site/en/consleg/2004/L/02004L0039-20060428-en.pdf FCA index for European Regulatory issues http://www.fca.org.uk/about/why-we-do-it/international/eu-directives
2	The firm's obligations for dealing fairly with clients and managing conflicts of interest	COBS Business obligations http://fshandbook.info/FS/html/FCA/COBS Conflicts of interest http://fshandbook.info/FS/html/FCA/SYSC/10 Unfair contract terms http://fshandbook.info/FS/html/FCA/UNFCOG FCA principles http://fshandbook.info/FS/html/FCA/PRIN
3	The regulatory requirements for	Client categorisation

	attracting, accepting, and providing information to clients	http://fshandbook.info/FS/html/FCA/COBS/3
		Communicating with clients, including financial promotions
		http://fshandbook.info/FS/html/FCA/COBS/4
		Distance communications
		http://fshandbook.info/FS/html/FCA/COBS/5
		Information about the firm, its services and remuneration
		http://fshandbook.info/FS/html/FCA/COBS/6
		Insurance mediation
		http://fshandbook.info/FS/html/FCA/COBS/7
		Client agreements
		http://fshandbook.info/FS/html/FCA/COBS/8
4	Elements of a compliant sales, advisory and discretionary management process	Suitability
		http://fshandbook.info/FS/html/FCA/COBS/9
		Appropriateness
		http://fshandbook.info/FS/html/FCA/COBS/10
		Dealing and managing
		http://fshandbook.info/FS/html/FCA/COBS/11
		Investment research
		http://fshandbook.info/FS/html/FCA/COBS/12
		Preparing product

		information
		http://fshandbook.info/FS/html/FCA/COBS/13
		Providing product information to clients
		http://fshandbook.info/FS/html/FCA/COBS/14
		Cancellation
		http://fshandbook.info/FS/html/FCA/COBS/15
5	Regulatory requirements governing post-sale client relationships	Reporting information to clients
		http://fshandbook.info/FS/html/FCA/COBS/16
		Client's assets
		http://fshandbook.info/FS/html/FCA/CASS
		Claims (long term care)
		http://fshandbook.info/FS/html/FCA/COBS/17
6	Requirements for the protection of clients in specific areas of regulatory activity involving higher risk or complexity	Pension products
		http://fshandbook.info/FS/html/FCA/COBS/19
		With profits
		http://fshandbook.info/FS/html/FCA/COBS/20
7	Regulatory requirements for the protection of client money and assets	Client's assets – custody, segregation, agreements, etc
		http://fshandbook.info/FS/html/FCA/CASS/1A
		http://fshandbook.info/FS/html/FCA/CASS/2

		http://fshandbook.info/FS/html/FCA/CASS/4
		http://fshandbook.info/FS/html/FCA/CASS/5
		http://fshandbook.info/FS/html/FCA/CASS/6
		http://fshandbook.info/FS/html/FCA/CASS/7
		http://fshandbook.info/FS/html/FCA/CASS/7a
		Client's assets – collateral
		http://fshandbook.info/FS/html/FCA/CASS/3
		Client's assets - mandates
		http://fshandbook.info/FS/html/FCA/CASS/8
8	Consumer Credit Act regulations	Consumer Credit Act
		http://fshandbook.info/FS/html/handbook/CONC

	Subject matter	Source material
1	Senior management arrangements, systems and controls. Corporate Governance and Outsourcing. Risk	SYSC - Senior management arrangements, systems and controls: http://fshandbook.info/FS/html/FCA/SYSC Senior Management General Requirements item 4.1.1 [R] http://fshandbook.info/FS/html/FCA/SYSC/4/1 Corporate Governance (Financial Reporting Council): http://www.frc.org.uk/corporate/combinedcode.cfm Outsourcing: http://fshandbook.info/FS/html/FCA/SYSC/8 Whistle blowing: http://fshandbook.info/FS/html/FCA/SYSC/18
2	Appointed Representatives And Agents	SUP – Supervision http://fshandbook.info/FS/html/FCA/SUP SYSC – Organisation; Employees and Agents http://fshandbook.info/FS/html/FCA/SYSC/5
3	Prudential Regulation including Capital Adequacy	Meeting Your Obligations http://www.fca.org.uk/firms/being-regulated/meeting-your-obligations

Regulatory Approach to Risk Management

		Prudential Regulation Handbooks
		http://fshandbook.info/FS/html/FCA/D166
		FCA - Financial Risk Outlook
		http://www.fca.org.uk/your-fca/documents/fca-risk-outlook
4	FCA Approach to Supervision	FCA general information
		http://www.fca.org.uk/about/what
		http://www.fca.org.uk/firms/markets/our-approach
		SUP – Supervision
		http://www.fca.org.uk/about/what/regulating/how-we-supervise-firms/our-approach-to-supervision
		http://fshandbook.info/FS/html/FCA/SUP
5	Training and Competence	TC – Training and Competence
		http://fshandbook.info/FS/html/FCA/TC
6	Financial Crime & Money Laundering	FCA general information Financial:
		http://fshandbook.info/FS/html/FCA/FC
		JMLSG – Joint Money Laundering Steering Group:
		http://www.jmlsg.org.uk/bba/jsp/polopoly.jsp;jsessionid=abBRz_wsohQ6?d=362&a=3424
	Market Abuse	MAR – Market conduct
		http://fshandbook.info/FS/html/FCA/MAR
7	Business Continuity	SYSC Senior Management

		requirements for business continuity http://fshandbook.info/FS/html/FCA/SYSC/4/1 item 4.1.6 R
8	Accounting Policies	SYSC requirements 4.1.9 R http://fshandbook.info/FS/html/FCA/SYSC/4/1
9	Regular Monitoring	Item 4.1.10 R http://fshandbook.info/FS/html/FCA/SYSC/4/1
10	FCA enforcement and disciplinary powers	FCA enforcing the law - general http://www.fca.org.uk/firms/being-regulated/enforcement EG - Enforcement Guide http://fshandbook.info/FS/html/FCA/EG Decision Procedure and Penalties Manual http://fshandbook.info/FS/html/FCA/DEPP FCA Statutory Panles http://www.fca.org.uk/about/governance/who/statutory-panels FCA Final notices with Search Facility http://www.fca.org.uk/your-fca/list?ttypes=Final+Notice&yyear=2013&ssearch=
11	Consumer Credit Act	Consumer Credit Act http://fshandbook.info/FS/html/handbook/CONC

Compliance and Ethics

	Subject matter	Source material
1	Role & objectives of the FCA	About the FCA
		http://www.fca.org.uk/about
		Aims and objectives
		http://www.fca.org.uk/about/why-we-do-it
2	Authorisation, permissions, the threshold conditions and perimeter guidance	Applying for Authorisation
		http://www.fca.org.uk/firms/about-authorisation/getting-authorised
		Important Changes to Authorisation
		http://www.fca.org.uk/firms/about-authorisation/important-changes
		COND – Threshold Conditions
		http://fshandbook.info/FS/html/FCA/COND
		PERG – Perimeter Guidance
		http://fshandbook.info/FS/html/FCA/PERG
		SUP – Supervision
		http://fshandbook.info/FS/html/FCA/SUP
		Being Regulated
		http://www.fca.org.uk/firms/being-regulated
3	New face of regulation	Human Face of Regulation
		http://www.fca.org.uk/news/speeches/human-face-of-regulation

4	The Principles for Businesses	FCA principles http://fshandbook.info/FS/html/FCA/PRIN
5	The fit and proper test for approved persons	FIT – The fit and proper test for approved persons http://fshandbook.info/FS/html/FCA/FIT
6	Statements of Principle and Code of Practice for Approved Persons	APER - Statements of Principle & Code of Practice for Approved Persons http://fshandbook.info/FS/html/FCA/APER
7	TCF and the compliance culture	"Handbook of Compliance", by Andrew Newton (published by Global Knowledge Solutions) FCA Treating Customer Fairly pages on website http://www.fca.org.uk/firms/being-regulated/meeting-your-obligations/fair-treatment-of-customers/who-tcf-applies-to Unfair contract terms http://fshandbook.info/FS/html/FCA/UNFCOG FCA principles http://fshandbook.info/FS/html/FCA/PRIN Training and TC – Training and Competence http://fshandbook.info/FS/ht

		ml/FCA/TC
8	Complaints and compensation	DISP – Dispute Resolution (Complaints)
		http://fshandbook.info/FS/html/FCA/DISPCOMP - Compensation
		http://fshandbook.info/FS/html/FCA/COMP
		Financial Ombudsman Service
		http://www.financial-ombudsman.org.uk/
		Financial Services Compensation Scheme
		http://www.fscs.org.uk/
9	Role of other regulatory bodies: - Office of Fair Trading - Information Commissioner	Office of Fair Trading
		http://www.oft.gov.uk/default.htm
		Information Commissioner
		http://www.ico.gov.uk/
10	Role of non statutory codes: - Lending Standards Board Code	Lending Standards Board
		http://www.lendingstandardsboard.org.uk/
		Lending Standards Board (Personal Code)
		http://www.lendingstandardsboard.org.uk/thecode.html
		Association of British Insurers
		http://www.abi.org.uk/

| 11 | UK Bribery Act 2010 | UK Bribery Act Guidance from the Ministry of Justice https://www.justice.gov.uk/legislation/bribery |

Anti-Money Laundering

	Subject matter	Source material
1	Role & objectives of the FCA	About the FCA http://www.fca.org.uk/about Aims and objectives http://www.fca.org.uk/about/why-we-do-it
2	FCA Principles for Businesses	PRIN – Principles for Businesses http://fshandbook.info/FS/html/FCA/PRIN
3	FCA Handbook – The UK Regulatory Approach	SYSC – Systems & Controls 3 – Financial Crime coverage http://fshandbook.info/FS/html/FCA/SYSC/3 SYSC – Systems & Controls 6 – Common Platform firms http://fshandbook.info/FS/html/FCA/SYSC/6
4	FCA - Market Conduct sourcebook	MAR – Market Conduct http://fshandbook.info/FS/html/FCA/MAR
5	FCA - Treating Customers Fairly	FCA Treating Customer Fairly pages on website http://www.fca.org.uk/firms/being-regulated/meeting-your-obligations/fair-treatment-of-customers/who-tcf-applies-to

6	FCA – Financial Crime	FCA general information Financial:
		http://fshandbook.info/FS/html/FCA/FC
		JMLSG – Joint Money Laundering Steering Group:
		http://www.jmlsg.org.uk/bba/jsp/polopoly.jsp;jsessionid=abBRz_wsohQ6?d=362&a=3424
		FCA general information - market abuse:
		http://www.fca.org.uk/firms/markets/market-abuse
7	Joint Money Laundering Steering Group (JMLSG) – UK Trade Association responsible for interpreting UK financial crime laws	JMLSG Website
		http://www.jmlsg.org.uk
		JMLSG Guidance Notes (main)
		http://www.jmlsg.org.uk/content/1/c4/68/86/Final_Part_I_030306.pdf
8	UK Financial crime law, policing & suspicious activity reporting	National Crime Agency (NCA)
		http://www.nationalcrimeagency.gov.uk/
		UK Assets Recovery Agency (now NCA)
		Proceeds of Crime Act 2002
		http://www.opsi.gov.uk/acts/acts2002/20020029.htm
		Money Laundering

		Regulations 2003 http://www.opsi.gov.uk/si/si2003/20033075.htm Money Laundering Regulations 2007 http://www.legislation.gov.uk/uksi/2007/2157/contents/made
9	Financial Action Task Force (FATF) – International inter-governmental body to develop and promote national & international policies	FATF Website. Also includes Non-Cooperative Countries & Territories (NCCT) http://www.fatf-gafi.org FATF 40 Recommendations. http://www.fatf-gafi.org/document/28/0,2340,en_32250379_32236930_33658140_1_1_1_1,00.html#40recs
10	Principles for Private Banking	The Wolfsberg Anti-Money Laundering Principles for Private Banking. http://www.wolfsberg-principles.com
11	Other International & National Links including sanctions controls	United Nations www.un.org/terrorism EU Sanctions http://ec.europa.eu/comm/external_relations/cfsp/s

			anctions/list/consol-list.htm
			Bank of England Sanctions
			http://www.bankofengland.co.uk/publications/financialsanctions/index.htm
			US Office of Foreign Assets Control
			www.ustreas.gov/offices/enforcement/ofac
			US Financial Crimes Enforcement Network
			www.fincen.gov
			Central Banks Website List
			http://www.bis.org/cbanks.htm
12	Trade Associations		http://www.mlro.net
13	General reading material		Relevant regulatory material such as FCA Consultation papers

PRA Links

	Subject matter	Source material
1	The role of the PRA	Essential facts about the PRA http://www.bankofengland.co.uk/pra/Pages/about/default.aspx
2	How firms are authorised to undertake regulated activities	About Authorisation http://www.bankofengland.co.uk/pra/Pages/authorisations/default.aspx Firm Types http://www.bankofengland.co.uk/pra/Pages/authorisations/newfirm/default.aspx Being regulated http://www.fca.org.uk/firms/being-regulated Markets http://www.fca.org.uk/firms/markets COND – Threshold Conditions http://fshandbook.info/FS/html/FCA/COND PERG – Perimeter Guidance http://fshandbook.info/FS/html/FCA/PERG Approved Persons http://www.bankofengland.co.uk/pra/Pages/authorisations/approvedpersons/default.aspx
3	CRD IV	CRD IV http://www.bankofengland.co.uk/pra/Pages/crdiv/default.aspx
4	How the PRA supervises firms and individuals	Supervision http://www.bankofengland.co.u

		k/pra/Pages/supervision/default.aspx
		Approved Persons http://www.bankofengland.co.uk/pra/Pages/authorisations/approvedpersons/default.aspx
5	Policy	PRA Policy http://www.bankofengland.co.uk/pra/Pages/policy/default.aspx
6	Publications	Publications from the PRA http://www.bankofengland.co.uk/pra/Pages/publications/default.aspx
7	Solvency II	Solvency II http://www.bankofengland.co.uk/pra/Pages/solvency2/default.aspx
8	Data Submission	Regulatory Data http://www.bankofengland.co.uk/pra/Pages/regulatorydata/default.aspx
9	News & Events	Latest News http://www.bankofengland.co.uk/pra/Pages/news/default.aspx

About The Author

Lee Werrell was born and grew up in Buckinghamshire, England and joined the Royal Navy in 1976. After 12 years and with a young family he ventured into the world of sales and then consultancy where he now runs a successful management consultancy (Compliance Consultant) that serves financial institutions nationwide in the UK.

Lee has also been heavily involved in Social Media and its use in Financial Services as well as providing a hobby for himself in his own passion, personal-development where he tries to help people identify and reach their potential. improveyourcondition.com

Married with two daughters and eight grandchildren there seems little time to do the finer things in life but Lee manages to find time for his writing. He says that he enjoys the thought that other people get a kick out of his stories and that is the satisfying part of being an author, coach and EBook friend that he tries to be.

Interact with the author; **Lee Werrell**

https://www.facebook.com/ComplianceDoctor

http://www.google.com/profiles/lee.werrell

http://wattpad.com/LeeWerrell

http://www.youtube.com/leewer100

uk.linkedin.com/leewerrell

Twitter

@leewerrell

@complianceconst

Printed in Great Britain
by Amazon.co.uk, Ltd.,
Marston Gate.